The Little Black Book of Fitness Business Success

The Little Black Book of Fitness Business Success

PAT RIGSBY

Foreword by: Nick Berry
Edited by: Timothy J. Ward

Fitness Consulting Group

Elizabethtown, KY

Disclaimer

The information in this book is for educational purposes only. There is an inherent risk assumed by any participant with any type of business activity. Those wishing or planning to partake in business activities should research their markets and understand the risks before doing so. The author of this book assumes no liability for any adverse outcomes. This is purely an educational book to educate those who are ready to take on such risks.

While the author has made every effort to provide accurate Internet addresses at the time of publication, the author does not assume any responsibility for errors or changes that occur after publication. Furthermore, the author does not have any control over and does not assume any responsibility for third-party websites or their content.

ISBN-13:
9780615466699

ISBN-10:
0615466699

Published in 2011 by Fitness Consulting Group

Cover design by Toby Brooks, NiTROhype Creative

Printed in the U.S.A.

Contents

Foreword

Throughout this book, you're going to read a lot about the sizzle and the steak. In the business coaching world, much like the rest of the world, it's not difficult to find the sizzle. Those who prefer the sizzle will happily seek you out so they can do what they do – sizzle – and not a great deal more.

Every once in a while though, you run into someone, and you recognize immediately that there's more to what they have to offer than just the sizzle – they deliver the steak as well. Pat is one of the rare people who happens to have some sizzle but also has a whole lot more of the steak.

The proof of what Pat brings is right there and easy to find. Wherever he's been, he has brought success, and he has brought it pretty quickly. As a college coach, he managed to take a program with the tiniest of budgets from an annual losing record to a national power in only a few years. He was the youngest college coach at any level to ever win 100 games. After coaching, he went into the fitness industry, and in a matter of months his region became a routine top producer for one of the largest personal training companies in the world. His success as a business owner in both the personal training and health club industries led him to the business coaching world and the birth of Fitness Consulting Group. Since its founding, FCG has exploded into multiple other ventures, including the franchises Athletic Revolution and Fitness Revolution, and the end results of all these ventures has been consistently the same: success.

I've been fortunate enough to have known and to have partnered with Pat since he's been in the fitness industry, so I have perspective on what he can accomplish like no one else can possibly have. There is an abundance of success stories and testimonials out there from individuals who can tell you of their results and experiences while working directly with him. However, I've been able to witness his impact over and over – instance after instance – year after year.

That just doesn't happen by accident. Success doesn't repeatedly materialize without the substance and formula behind it. That's the thing about Pat, and that's what you'll find in this book; he knows what is needed to be successful, and he can teach you to blend those "ingredients". Whether it's mastering your service, marketing, staffing, etc., he knows how to transform your business into a successful operation. He has proven it time and time again, and I trust that he will continue to do so – to the benefit of thousands and thousands of fitness professionals as well as to our own companies.

-Nick Berry

Introduction

During my time in the fitness industry, I have watched many people aspire to success. I am one of those people, and while I'm certainly a work in progress, my business partner Nick Berry and I have had our fair share of success already and also have helped thousands of fitness pros just like you achieve great successes of their own.

Because of this I'm often asked what my "secrets" to success are. I don't think they're secrets, but every one of us needs to have a formula that works on a personal level. This book is a collection of essays that share the strategies, tactics, and the mindset 'secrets' that have led us and the fitness professionals we have worked with to the successes that we've achieved and that will undoubtedly be the foundation for our future successes.

Here are my suggestions on how to use this book. I've written each chapter so that it can stand on it's own as a lesson that you can take immediate action on, so don't feel that you have to read the entire book before you can start deriving benefit from it. Read a chapter, and apply what you've learned. Take action. If you approach the book in this fashion, I can guarantee that you will benefit greatly from this resource. The lessons in *The Little Black Book of Fitness Business Success* have helped personal trainers and coaches open their own facilities, grow six and seven figure a year businesses, enjoy more freedom, and enjoy the types of careers and lives they've always wanted – and these lessons can do the same for you too.

Dedicated To Your Success,

Pat Rigsby

Client Getting Made Simple

If you want to accomplish anything, basically it boils down to this simple formula:

1. Set A target

2. Break down reaching that target into a few simple steps

Let's use getting more clients as an example.

Target: Get 10 New Clients In August

Step 1: Ask every current client for the names and contact information of 3 prospects in exchange for a branded T-shirt.

Step 2: Contact each of those prospects and offer them a free sample of what you do.

Step 3: Contact all former clients and offer them an incentive to start back with you.

Step 4: Attend at least 4 networking events in August, and add at least 3 people to your network at each.

Step 5: Offer those 12 people a free sample of what you do.

With that simple approach you should be able to get a minimum of 20 prospects in for a free trial or a couple free sessions. Of those you should have no problem converting at least half, and you will have your 10.

Now maybe you prefer public speaking or Facebook ads. Maybe you prefer the *Business of the Month* program. That's OK – the formula is the same. The key is being specific.

Set a specific target, and create simple but specific steps.

In the example I specified how many clients I wanted to get (10).

I specified how many clients I'd ask for referrals (all of them).

I specified how many leads I'd ask for from each client (3).

I specified how many former clients I'd contact (all of them).

Finally, I specified how many networking events I'd go to (4) and how many leads I'd get from each one (3).

This approach not only gives me a goal for each step, but also it allows me to measure, which, in turn, allows me to improve moving forward.

If I determine that many of my clients wouldn't give me 3 leads, for example, that would mean that I needed a stronger incentive.

If I figure out that very few of my former clients are willing to come back in, I need a better offer.

If I learn that I'm only getting 2 new contacts at each networking event, I need to attend more events.

If I close fewer than half the trials, I need to tighten up my sales presentation, or I need to make the trial a better experience for the prospect.

If you're not being specific, you'll never figure out any of this. You'll be stuck just guessing what you need to do next.

So set a target and some simple but specific steps to get there, and you'll suddenly see the business side of what you do get easier and your number of clients grow month after month.

21 Thoughts for Building a Bulletproof Fitness Business

1. Break out of the fitness industry norms – the majority is almost always wrong and are always behind.

2. Recycle what you do. Deliver the same content in different formats. Fitness coaching programs, infoproducts, bootcamps to go – they're all the same stuff packaged in different formats.

3. Small hinges swing big doors. A few small but strategic changes can make big differences to the bottom line.

4. A different way to look at your market is to find price gaps instead of pricing the way everyone else does. If you can get a health club membership for $39, a bootcamp membership for $199, and 1 on 1 personal training for $500, then the gaps are $99 and $299-399. What can you offer there?

5. Joining the Chamber of Commerce is like joining a gym. Most people won't do anything with their memberships, but if you take advantage of what they offer, joining can be a huge difference maker.

6. If you have no money – knock on doors, hustle, network, and make something happen every day. Roll up your sleeves, and go to work. You can overcome a lack of money with an abundance of hustle in most areas.

7. Successful people have a sense of urgency. Procrastination is not acceptable.

8. If you accept mediocrity, you will get more of it. Mediocrity only exists if you tolerate it, so stop tolerating it.

9. People mess up joint ventures and referrals by not making it easy for others to help them. Help them help you. Do as much of the work as possible for them, and you'll get 10X the results.

10. Are you the first person in your market that people think of when it comes to what you do? If not, re-define what you do, or tighten down your niche.

11. The quickest way to more money is to sell more to your current clients. Do you offer supplements, workshops, weight management, higher priced coaching, etc?

12. You decide. You decide how people view you and your business. You decide what hours you are going to work. You decide how you are going to live your life. If you don't decide, someone else will decide for you.

13. There is hidden opportunity in every business. Three easy ones are upsells from your basic

programs, downsells for people who don't buy, and reactivation of previous clients. It's money that's just sitting there waiting for you to grab it.

14. Associate with like minded, successful people. It's often said that your income is the average of the 5 people's incomes you're around most, so don't hang out with slackers.

15. If most people realized that they had all the same skills (often better) as the top earning trainers in the field, there would be a LOT more six-figure earners in our industry.

16. A big obstacle to success is distraction. Turn off the email and TV, and work on your business.

17. Always have a higher priced option. There are a certain number of people in a market who will pay top price.

18. Work on yourself as much as your business.

19. It's not what you make; it's what you keep. Focus on improving your net profits.

20. Organize your day the night before. Block off time for everything important to you. Working on your business gets time. Networking gets time. Family gets time. Self improvement gets time. If you don't schedule it, you'll put it off.

21. A lot of success is born out of a hatred of losing. As a coach I enjoyed winning, but I HATED losing.

The X Factor for
Fitness Business Success

If you really want to know the thing that allows some people to enjoy success while others settle for mediocrity, I'll tell you. It's pretty simple.

Drive.

If one of your clients wants to lose weight, it's more about their want, desire and willingness to stick to your program than it is about having a magic system.

If you want to build a six or seven figure business, it's more about your hunger and willingness to do what most won't than it is about the latest and greatest marketing fad or client getting system.

The truth is, a lot of different approaches will work…

…If you will.

I can look back and see this clearly hold true in pretty much any success I've ever had and for all the successful people I've known.

When I became a baseball coach, the two previous coaches at that university had been a former Major

League All-Star and a legendary high school coach that had made the jump to coaching at the collegiate level.

Both struggled in the job I was about to take, and both had tons more experience, credentials, and resources.

I was 23, and I can look back and count on one hand the number of people that expected me to be even modestly successful, and that's including myself.

But the fear of failure drove me tirelessly. With less experience, worse facilities, and poorer resources than virtually everyone we competed against, I was able to be successful because I was willing to do what others wouldn't.

When other coaches were vacationing during the summer, I was working.

When they were home, I was recruiting.

While they were comfortable, I was hungry.

Really, I was just unwilling to fail, and it drove me constantly.

When I moved into the business world, I'd only read 4 books that could be considered 'business books' in my life, I'd never made more than $33,000 in a year, and I'm pretty sure I was about as unprepared for success as someone could be.

But after taking about 18 months to work for someone to learn the ropes of the industry and study up on business, I took the leap into entrepreneurship and I, along with my business partner Nick, started a business. But this time that *drive,* and also that fear of failure, was even bigger.

At that point, everyone I'd known in my life thought of me as a baseball coach and always expected me to go back to that. So that fear of failure gnawed at me again. But there was a second driver that wouldn't let me fail. Family.

When we got started, my wife Holly, my step son Tyler, and I lived in a basement for a year, and under no circumstances was I going to fail them. Almost everyone has their stories like this where they struggled and paid their dues.

It's just that most of them aren't in their early thirties. But, that was the choice I'd made since I'd decided to change careers mid-stream, and as far as I was concerned, failure was not an option.

Looking back upon both cases, I (or Nick and I on the second situation) had a lot fewer resources and lesser experience than the competition. But that was made up for with drive.

However, this drive, this willingness to do what others will not, is hardly exclusive to me.

Nick was willing to do what it took to become the industry's leading expert in the "backside" of fitness businesses – and I'm pretty sure that's not where his passion started out since his degree is in Exercise Science, and he started as a trainer – not a business guy. But he was willing to dive into the part of business that most in the industry (including myself) prefer to delegate, outsource or ignore.

It seems like everyone talks about wanting to start their own info-empire at one point or another, but few are willing to put in the time once they realize it's a full time job too.

Holly works more hours with her business *Fit Yummy Mummy* than she did when ran all our weight management programs, but that drive has allowed her to build a great business when most would've quit.

A.J. Roberts and his wife moved across the country to work at our gym here in Kentucky because he wanted to be part of our team. When he saw that we needed help with certain online tasks, he volunteered to take them on before he knew how to do them – then went and studied up in a hurry – because he was driven to make more money and move up the ladder with us. Now, because of this drive, he has positioned himself as one of the leading experts in the industry when it comes to all things online.

Almost all successful people have their own stories like these, and we're fortunate enough to work with a LOT of successful business owners who use different business models, different marketing strategies, and even different training methods.

But the one thing you'll find in all of them – and every other successful person – is drive.

3 Killer Referral Strategies

Physician Referrals: If you want to set yourself apart from other fitness pros in your community, send a health and fitness report to your clients' physicians. This professional courtesy is designed to create a line of communication between the doctor and yourself – and as a bonus, it positions you as a credible resource for the doctor when making recommendations to patients. The report might include the following:

- Weight
- Bodyfat Percentage
- Resting Heart Rate
- Blood Pressure
- Muscular Strength Assessment
- Flexibility/Mobility Assessment

Include whatever else goes into your assessment process. You can send this report each time you update your assessment. This single approach can set you apart from other fitness pros and fitness providers in the eyes of your community's medical professional.

Referral Stimulator Email: This is very simple to do. Just send a personal email to clients and ask for referrals. Here's an example:

Subj: *I Need Your Help!*

Dear Ms. Jones,

I think you can help me with a problem I have. I don't know if you realize it or not, but marketing for new clients can be pretty expensive. And after I spend all that money on marketing, I'm still not guaranteed to get one single new client.

"Word of Mouth" marketing is still the best type of marketing. And frankly, I'd rather reward you for sending me new clients than spend all my money on radio or newspaper. Many happy clients have mentioned that their friends, acquaintances, and family members have expressed an interest in improving their health and fitness. With this in mind, I came up with my new...

Referral Reward Program!

Here's how it works. For every referral that you send me who becomes a client, I'll give you 20% off of your monthly rate for the next 3 months.

So if you refer just 5 people you'll get your next 3 months of training FREE!

I know that I don't have to offer rewards for referring friends, but I think it's important to show that I value you as a client and appreciate your referrals.

When you think about people that you might refer, keep these ideas in MIND:

- *People you work with*
- *Friends listed in your phone or email address book*
- *Neighbors*
- *People you know from your hobbies and other interests*
- *Family members*
- *People you do business with*
- *People who attend your church*

Hopefully, that will jog your memory a little. If you just spend a few minutes thinking about it, I'm sure you'll come up with quite a few people you know who would like to experience all the benefits that you've experienced while working with me.

All you need to do is reply with the people you think would be interested in finding out more about my services and their contact information. I'll contact them and offer them a free gift of 2 weeks of my fitness bootcamp as a gift from you.

Thanks for your help and I look forward to rewarding you soon!

"Bring a Friend" Sessions: If you run bootcamps, this is the most simple referral system you can put in place. Just announce a "Bring A Friend Week" in which all of your clients can bring a guest free of charge to participate in a week of workouts.

Announce the event about a week prior to the actual day, and continue to promote it leading up to the event. You can combine this with another referral system and offer incentives or a preferred rate for any guest that becomes a client. Have a way to capture the contact information of each guest and continue to market to them via a newsletter or other promotional material. Have a free report and a special offer for upcoming events available to them at the conclusion of the session.

This works almost as well with standard one-on-one or semi-private training, it just takes a little more preparation for the actual sessions. You can develop a standardized entry-level program for the guests to follow for their workouts.

If you want to really take this to the next level, hold a contest with prizes for the camper or client that brings the most friends during the week, and give them their next month free.

Now you have 3 easy to use referral strategies at your disposal. Pick 2 and plug them into your business next week so you can start getting these referrals rolling in.

3 Fitness Sales
Keys To Remember

Selling personal training, bootcamps, youth fitness programs, or even health club memberships... that is the foundation of your business. No sale means no client, camper or member.

But most fitness pros I know hate selling, but that's only because they're not comfortable with it yet. Here are three tips to change that and make closing sales much, much easier.

Fitness Sales Key #1 – Everything Leads To A Sale

Sometimes I have to remind the trainers we work with that while sending press releases, getting on TV, making blog posts, writing articles, and creating products are great...they're all just a means to lead to you selling something.

See, sometimes we have to keep our eyes on the prize. Let's say you don't have enough clients or campers. What are you going to do? Are you the type of person that will simply wait around for something to happen...or are you the person that will you go out and make it happen?

When Holly and I were living in a basement while we were getting our training business and health club ramped up, I was laser focused on selling training. I didn't leave the gym without getting two new clients. It meant some late nights, but like they say, when there's a will, there's a way.

Even before that, when I was first running a training department in a local gym, the company had a bonus of $250 if you sold 12 deals in a pay period. My goal every pay period was 36 deals, and I considered that $750 part of my regular income. I knew I needed 3 deals a day to make it happen and was relentless on getting those three. So, you can keep doing all those other things... blogging, sending press releases, writing articles, etc. But don't lose sight of the fact that selling is what pays the bills.

Fitness Sales Key #2 – Proper Framing Leads To Bigger Sales

Want an easy way to sell bigger deals? It's two simple steps, but I'm not sure you'll believe me if I tell you.

Step 1: Offer no more than 3 potential options to a prospect... something like this:

> ➢ 1 Session Per Week

> ➢ 2 Sessions Per Week

> ➢ 3 Sessions Per Week

It could be 2, 3 and 4, or it could be 3, 4 and 5. It makes no difference really. You know what you're currently selling. Just reduce it to 3 options.

Step 2: If your most popular program is 2 sessions per week but you want to sell more 3 session per week packages, add a package bigger than that to your price sheet.

If you already have:

> 1 Session Per Week

> 2 Sessions Per Week

> 3 Sessions Per Week

Then switch to offering:

> 2 Sessions Per Week

> 3 Sessions Per Week

> 4 Sessions Per Week

You'll immediately sell more 3 session per week programs. It's all simple psychology. Too many choices have been proven to cause indecision, and high priced offerings make offerings priced lower seem more reasonable. There you have it, two easy steps to more sales, bigger packages, and more programs sold.

Fitness Sales Key #3 – Sell Something

Get small commitments first.There was a time in my personal training career that I'd average three closed sales a day. Unfortunately many trainers don't do 3 a month. The trick was to close the ones that weren't ready to commit to bigger programs on something smaller.

19

If I was doing a speaking engagement, I'd close the attendees on something small. Get a 'yes' first. Once someone has invested a little with you, it's much, much easier to get them to invest more... but only if you deliver great service during that initial purchase.

So if you're having trouble getting people to enroll in "big ticket" programs, get them to at least invest in something small first.

Then after you've built a little more rapport and have delivered great service and value, present your bigger offerings.

You'll be pleasantly surprised at how little resistance you get then.

This should help you get a little more confident and comfortable with sales.

5 Proven Fitness Referral Strategies Guaranteed To Bring In Clients

As far as I'm concerned, referrals should be at the core of any good fitness pro's marketing system. The only problem is that using the same referral strategy over and over can get stale fast – so here are five ways you can keep the referrals coming in without sounding like a broken record.

Fitness Referral Strategy #1: Make it a Condition of Doing Business

Description: Make it a mandatory part of being your client. I know – it sounds easier said than done – but hear me out. This is especially effective if you have an in-demand service. State from the onset, as a condition of working with you, that clients each need to refer 2 friends. Obviously, you have to be tactful about it.

Here's an example of what you could say:

"If I do everything I've promised and you lose those 20 unwanted pounds, will you provide me with 2 referrals of friends, co-workers or family members that could use the same benefits?"

So, at the very beginning, your clients will know what they're in for.

Fitness Referral Strategy #2: Your Community's Best Businesses

Description: What you do is compile a list of other types of businesses that also serve your ideal client. After you've developed a comprehensive list of these types businesses, search through your database of clients, friends, and contacts for people that operate businesses in these categories. If there are business categories that you have no contacts with, look for a mutual friend that can serve as a liaison to a successful professional in that category.

Now rank the professionals in each category as to which you'd prefer to affiliate yourself and your business with most. Send the "Tier 1" professionals a letter suggesting that you'd like to invite them to be a member of "Your Community's Best Businesses" and receive referrals from several of the other premier professionals in the community. Let them know that your goal is to create a network of the best local professionals in hopes of best serving each member's customers or clients and providing high quality referrals for the members.

This group would meet once a month and you would serve as the host/leader (another way of subtly enhancing your perception among group members). Each member would be able to present for 10-15 minutes as a means of educating the group about their business and how it would be of benefit to their customers/clients. Each member can make special offers to customers/clients of fellow group members, do endorsed mailings, etc. To increase the perception of this group, you could launch a website (youtownsbestbusinesses.com), do a newsletter, or provide testimonials from all of the happy, cross-referred customers.

This involves a little more work than most fitness referral strategies, but done well, it could easily provide you with more business than you could ever handle.

Fitness Referral Strategy #3: "Thank You" Gift Cards

Description: After a meaningful moment during a client's time with you – perhaps after they've met a goal or finished a 12 week program – hand them 3 plastic gift cards and tell say, "Here are 3 gift cards that you can give to friends, co-workers, or family members that would like to enjoy the same results that you have. It entitles them to get $100 off our (name of program) program as a gift from you. And as a way of saying thank you for being such a great client I want to give you $X off of your next program as well."

Fitness Referral Strategy #4: "Thank You" Postcards

Description: Similar to the "Thank You" gift cards – after a meaningful moment during a client's time with you, hand them 2-3 pre-printed and stamped postcards that detail a special offer and say, "Here are 3 postcards that you can address to people important to you that you'd like to see benefit from changes similar to the one's you've made. It entitles them to get $50 off our (name of program) program as a gift from you. Simply address each postcard to someone important to you and sign them, and I'll be happy to put them in the mail. And as a way of saying thank you for being such a great client I want to give you $X off of your next program as well."

Both of these "thank you" strategies can be very powerful, but make sure that your client gets the credit for the gifts they give. If they don't get something out of giving the gifts, they're highly unlikely to give them. So when a gift card comes in, be sure to ask who provided the new prospect with the card.

Fitness Referral Strategy #5: Send a Gift To Work

Description: This is a great method to use, especially if your client has just graduated from a program you offer or achieved a specific goal. Send a big bouquet of balloons to your client's work congratulating them on their success. The balloons don't need to have any logo or writing on them… they just need to have a card congratulating the client on their success.

What will happen is that everyone at the client's place of work will ask who the balloons are from. The client will tell everyone about you and how much you've helped them. The balloons act as a talking point about how happy the client is with their trainer (you).

The Right Way to Run a Business

Every year, I attend at least one Perform Better Functional Training Summit. Every time I'm at one of these events, I think about how much fitness professionals could learn from the Perform Better company, so I decided to share some lessons I've taken away from doing business with them which could benefit all of our businesses:

- **Deliver Value To Grow Your Business**– I've attended about 10 Perform Better events, and every time I've felt like I've gotten more than my money's worth. In fact, to this point I've yet to come across someone who didn't feel like they've received their money's worth (or more) at any of the Perform Better events.

This kind of consistent value that they deliver is the foundation of their success and should be the foundation of any business's success. It's as simple as this: In every transaction you have with a customer or client, it is your job to provide them with an experience that makes them want to do business with you again.

- **Educate and the Sales Will Come**– The Perform Better Summits, the Functional Movement Screen Workshops, and all the other Perform Better events are all incredible sales vehicles despite nobody ever really "pitching" anything. The key is simple. Each of these events educates fitness professionals on how they can do a better job serving their clients. This is a great way to generate sales in two ways:

  1. Any of the tools or resources used in the presentations are made available by Perform Better, so if fitness professionals want to implement what they've learned, Perform Better offers solutions so they can.

  2. The fitness industry is notorious for turnover so by educating fitness professionals, Perform Better is essentially helping people stay in the industry, become more successful, and in turn, potentially become a long term customer.

How can you apply this? The more informed your clients are, the more successful they will be. If you educate them on nutrition, supplements, and a supportive lifestyle, they'll be more likely to reach their goals and will be more likely to stay with you as a client. Not only that, but since they will be more educated, they will seek out these other solutions like supplements or nutrition education, which you can provide for them as an additional profit center.

- **Make Everything A Win / Win–** This is similar to my first point, but we deal with Perform Better on a bit of a different level than most consumers (we offer a pre-conference IYCA Certification Workshop and have done a few other things with them outside of simply attending events or making purchases).

What I've consistently seen from them is that in every transaction, every project, and in every working relationship, they work to make sure that both parties come out ahead.

This sounds simple, but in business and especially in the fitness industry, it's not as common as it should be.

They've worked diligently to make sure we benefit at every turn when we deal with them, and you should be doing the same in all your business relationships. You should make it a goal that every client, prospect, JV partner, or member of your network feels like when they deal with you, they benefit.

- **Keep Evolving–** Every year Perform Better Summits keep changing and improving. Each year there are new presentations highlighting the latest successful industry trends in training and equipment. In fact, the Summits are often the vehicle to educate fitness professionals on the latest industry developments, so they're usually the people setting the tone for a lot of what successful trainers and coaches are doing with their clients.

- **Use Relationships As Your Foundation–** We talk about it over and over, and Perform Better is a perfect example of it – relationships are crucial to business success.

When I attend Perform Better events it feels kind of like a big family reunion – but more fun.

This isn't an accident. Their team is incredible and takes a personal interest in everyone they do business with. In fact, it's pretty apparent in everything that they do from consistently looking for ways for you (or us) to save money when making purchases to little things like Chris Poirier – taking a couple minutes out from running the event – to have an I-Phone Lightsaber battle with Tyler.

In fact, the rep that we work with, Jennie Rohde had a baby gift for Holly and me when we showed up. How thoughtful is that?

All of this is stuff you can do as well. Take a personal interest in your clients. Be nice (and attentive) to their kids. Go out of your way to help them be more successful.

There you go – 5 big lessons you can take away from the equipment company I consider to be far and away the leader in serving the fitness professional market.

21 Fitness Business Proverbs

Here are 21 different ways you can grow your business – all you need to do is pick one or two of them and apply them to your business. So get to picking...

1. Offer strong guarantees. The stronger the better.

2. Have an upsell for everything. A minimum of 20% will take it.

3. Make it easy to buy.

4. Use EFT... 95% of people pay things monthly.

5. Find ways to get people on recurring programs.

6. Add down sells to convert more prospects.

7. Sizzle is fine in marketing, but education is better.

8. A transaction is the beginning of a relationship, not the end of one.

9. Find the void in a market – then fill it.

10. Relationship marketing trumps all other types of marketing.

11. Opportunities are endless, but you can't act on them all at once.

12. Treat prospects like clients and clients like family.

13. Public speaking and webinars are under used tools.

14. Scarcity creates action.

15. Give to get. If you treat people well, you'll be paid back 10X over.

16. The better the follow up, the better the business.

17. There is **at least** 10K hiding in every business. Most people never look for it. Start by looking for it.

18. Price is elastic... have you checked how far yours can stretch?

19. Combine what you already have or offer, and then create new things to sell.

20. Don't step over dollars to pick up pennies.

21. If you don't believe it can and will happen...it won't happen.

A Fitness Coaching Program
Guaranteed To Make You Money

Here is a ready to go fitness coaching program you can plug into your business to sell to former clients, unconverted leads, and prospects that can't afford your base programs.

Schedule: You're going to meet with a group either once a week or once every two weeks. Up to you. Ultra-successful trainer Brian Calkins ran a program like this very successfully, and his groups met every two weeks. My wife Holly ran one that sold out consistently, and their group met every week.

The program can be 4 weeks, 8 weeks, 12 weeks or 16 weeks. That is entirely up to you. Brian held his for 16 weeks, while Holly did hers for 4 weeks. Many programs will work. If I were recommending what I think would work best, I'd go with running a 12 week program.

Each session will last roughly 60-90 minutes. You cover a nutrition lesson for the first 30 minutes and a workout they can do at home the next 30 minutes. If you build in time to troubleshoot and answer questions, you're probably looking at 90 minutes.

m: We used weekly nutrition lessons for ran that you can find for free in the section at *nutritionmoneymachine.com*. The weight management program is there, and you can use that as is, or if you have a different system that you adhere to, just make sure it's broken up into lessons.

For the workouts, the simplest way to go is to teach everyone a workout they can do at home using bodyweight, dumbbell, and band exercises. Good examples of these types of programs are Holly's *Fit Yummy Mummy* program, *Turbulence Training*, and Alwyn Cosgrove's *Afterburn* program. I'm sure you can create a series of workouts that fits this mold.

You do need to make sure there are progressions and regressions so that all participants can follow what you're providing.

Money: I think the magic in a program like this is that you can offer it for less than $100 per month, and people won't feel like they're going to be reliant on a trainer for life. If you do a 12 week program, you could sell it for $79-99 per month for 3 months. Collect the first payment at enrollment, and set the next 2 up on whatever automated payment system you use. Then you'll be all set.

Details/Considerations: You need to position this as a coaching program. It's not personal training, and it's not a bootcamp. Not only do the prospects you're marketing this to need to know it, but also your current clients need to as well so that they don't feel like you're offering something really similar to what they are purchasing at a discounted price.

This program is about empowerment and education, not daily motivation and accountability.

One other consideration is that because this is a group program, you need a place to do it. Most places you'd hold a bootcamp work. Just remember, there is a nutrition component where the participants will probably be sitting down. If you do in home training, you'll need a location where a group can meet.

Marketing: I'd go to all former clients and missed sales first. Either call them or send them a letter and follow with a call. Tell them about your new program that would be perfect for them!

After that, I'd use this as a downsell for any prospect you meet with that doesn't purchase your main offering(s).

Wrapping It Up: This type of program really is pretty simple to execute. The nutrition lessons are already done for you if you use that website I listed earlier. I'm sure you can come up with solid workouts, but if you're lazy, drop $39.95 and buy one of the ones I mentioned or any other program that can be executed at home.

Then you just need to identify where you're going to hold the program and set a launch date.

Start marketing and you're all set!

How much can you make? I can't say for sure. It depends on the number of people you have in your database for starters. But I'd be amazed if you couldn't fill up at least one group of 10. If that's all you do, that's an additional $800-1000 per month for 6 hours of work. If you have more time or other trainers working for you...the sky is the limit.

14 Surefire Ways To Grow Your Fitness Business

1. **Be Great At What You Do–** If you're a terrible trainer or coach, all the marketing advice in the world won't make up for it. Think about seeing a great ad for a restaurant. It might get you in the door for one meal, but if your meal was bad, would any amount of advertising ever get you back?

2. **Joint Ventures–** Have you ever taken the time to find out how many businesses are there in your area who serve your potential clientele? You should. Build a relationship with them so you can eventually have them as a referral source. Start by being nice, offering free training to the owners and at least steep discounts to the staff. Send them some referrals. Eventually you will be able to get referrals and evem more structured lead generation activities in return like endorsed mailings or emails.

3. **Public Speaking–** Incredible business builder. Why sell to one person when you can sell to 20, 30, 50, 100, or more at one time while also being

positioned as an expert. There is no shortage of groups, clubs, and organizations looking for speakers, so don't ignore what is probably the best lead generation opportunity available to you.

4. **Reactivating Old Clients and Old Prospects–** These people already know you and have shown an interest in what you offer. Some of them have even worked with you. Go back to them with a special offer, and grow your business.

5. **Networking–** There is nothing better than face to face marketing. There is no postcard, e-mail, or newspaper ad that can compare to talking to someone in person. *Make a point of meeting several new people each day and adding them to your personal network.* Get out from behind the computer, attend networking events, and put yourself in more settings with people outside of your inner circle.

6. **Up Sells and Backend Sales–** There is NO ONE better to sell to than your current clients. If someone is purchasing a training program from you, *make them an offer at the point of sale* and upgrade them to a nutritional coaching program, a supplement package, or an accelerated training program that will compliment what they've already purchased. Don't hesitate to create new stuff to sell to the same people that have been buying from you for a while. You'd be amazed at some clients appetites for new offers.

7. **Hustle–** Nothing gets done without hustle. We regularly host live business coaching events such as Bootcamp Bootcamp, and many of our star students regularly attend. They come from different parts of the country (even other parts of the world), and some have facilities while others don't. Each of them have honed in on 2-3 core strategies that have built their businesses – and it's a different 2-3 for many of them.

   But the one thing that is the same for all of them is that they hustle!

8. **Social Proof–** You can never have too many testimonials. It is a great way to recognize clients' successes, and you never know which one will resonate with the prospect you're talking to, so have a lot.

9. **Referrals–** You should make referral generation your key marketing strategy. It only takes 4 things to make this happen. 1) A great service that people want to share. 2) You asking for referrals from EVERYONE– no exceptions. 3) You making it super-easy to refer prospects to you. 4) You rewarding people for directing prospects to you.

   That's it, and as you noticed, the burden falls squarely on you, not your clients.

10. **Risk Reversal–** There should be zero risk for someone to do business with you. Free trials, 100% or more money back guarantees, short term

entryway programs like a 21 Day Drop a Dress Size programs – they're all great ways to eliminate the risk for the prospect.

11. **Invest In Yourself** – Go to events like Perform Better Summits and Bootcamp Bootcamp. Invest in educational products and programs, and get a business coach or mentor.

    In fact, I don't know any successful fitness pros who haven't gotten some form of coaching or who haven't belonged to a mastermind group. That's not an accident.

12. **EFT Billing**- You didn't get into this business to be a bill collector, did you?

13. **Sell Memberships, Not Sessions**– Too many trainers sell a series, blocks, or packages– all a bunch of short term offerings that make it tougher to have a sustainable business with steady cash flow. Don't be one of them.

    Sell your programs as monthly memberships where clients invest a set amount each month for a defined amount of service. Ideally this membership will be for a commitment of several (or more) months or will at least auto-renew every month.

14. **Care About Your People**– Your clients. Your network. Your staff. Make it readily apparent that you care about them and their success every chance you get.

In general, people are willing to pay more for anything just to give in to a desire for convenience.

The old Chinese Proverb goes like this:

Give a man a fish and you feed him for a day. Teach a man to fish and you feed him for a lifetime.

But most people don't want to learn to fish.

They want you to catch the fish, clean it, cook it and serve it to them.

The more you do for them – the happier they are.

They don't want to make decisions. They are busy. They're bombarded with information and choices, so the simpler you make it and the more you do for them, the better your business will be.

Done-for-you can be as small as Lunchables at the grocery store or as big as a franchise like Athletic Revolution.

But the one thing in common is that it's designed to make things easier for the customer or client.

can you integrate done-for-you into your ,onal training business for more profits?

Here are a few ideas:

Offer More Training Programs– My friend and mentorship client offers a running club that his bootcampers can join (for a fee) on their non-camp days. You could offer something like this or a different type of class that compliments your main program. Another friend and coaching client, Bob McEnaney, is an avid cyclist and has created a group cycling program. Group interval training is an easy option you could add. Just pick something that your clients would be interested in and that compliments what they are already doing.

Offer A Kitchen Makeover– Instead of just educating clients on proper nutrition, charge a fee to go to a client's home, clean out the kitchen, and restock it with supportive food and supplements. You're eliminating all the guesswork for them and increasing the likelihood for their success.

Offer Meal Plans– This is the easiest of the bunch and can provide substantial back end profits. You can sell or give (if you want to build it into your program to add value) clients something as simple as a 7-14 day cleanse-type program to get clients off on the right foot or something as elaborate as a complete meal plan collection for each month.

Imagine how much easier you will be making your clients' lives if you provide meal plans, recipes, shopping lists, and your recommended supplement program. In fact, that's an easy way to make offering meal plans much more lucrative for you: build recommended supplementation into the meal plans. If you ever saw the recommended meal plans in the bestseller *Body For Life*, they integrated meal replacement shakes and various other supplements – not coincidentally all from the EAS product line.

Think it sold some product for them?

If you sell any supplements, this is a no brainer.

Offer Information Products– Holly has her new Fit Yummy Mummy Transformation Kit, which is a follow-along collection of DVDs and other done-for-you components designed to make following her Fit Yummy Mummy program as easy as possible.

Think about why the P90X program is so popular. It isn't because the training program is spectacular or revolutionary. It is because all you have to do if you buy it is follow along. Most people don't want to learn about the "whys" – they just want to be told what to do.

You could offer something to your current clients or campers that compliments what they do with you. You could also do what bootcamp guru BJ Gaddour has done and develop a "Bootcamp to Go" for the people that want to work with you but may not be able to afford the in-person offerings or might live too far away to participate. Basically, there are a lot of different ingredients that go into your clients' (and potential clients') fitness regimens. The more of them that you can address with a done-for-you solution, the happier your clients will be – and the more they'll be willing to pay.

The Truth About
Fitness Business Success

Are you creating a success that you're going to enjoy?

I know it sounds strange to ask if you're going to enjoy success – but bear with me for a few minutes and you'll see what I'm getting at.

On one of the trips Nick and I made to Perform Better in Providence, Rhode Island, we got to see lots of friends and colleagues – plus we got to head down to Pembroke, Massachusetts to visit Athletic Revolution franchisees Dave & Andrea Gleason.

Hanging out with guys like Pat Beith, Eric Cressey, Mike Boyle, the Gleasons, and Alwyn Cosgrove is not only a great time but always thought provoking.

One of the things Alwyn and I were chatting about was how much traveling he was doing and how it was wearing on him a bit. He's one of the most in demand speakers in the industry (If you've ever heard him talk, you know why – he's awesome) – but his speaking schedule has expanded so much that he's getting on a plane about every 8 days on average. He's basically become so successful at this that so much travel is making it less enjoyable.

So right now Alwyn is developing his plan to make this part of what he does serve him better.

It reminded me of when Nick and I initially planned on opening about a dozen health clubs. We had 2 locations and were about to sign a lease on a third, but knowing how much time and energy each one would have required – it would have been years and years before we would have ever really been able to enjoy the fruits of our efforts.

Personally, the health club side of our businesses was not what I enjoyed the most, not by a long shot. And the thought of being on the road every day to visit the clubs and being away from my family that much was not the type of success I was looking for.

So instead, we changed gears and started shifting our business interests to things we loved doing and that were congruent with the lifestyles we wanted to have.

Getting to catch up with Eric Cressey just reminded me again of how important this concept is.

Eric is an incredible coach and could probably expand his business to serve any market he wanted to. He gets opportunities to expand the Cressey Performance brand into other locations.

But Eric has carved out a position as having one of the best, if not the best, baseball performance facilities in the world, and he is loving every minute of it.

Sure, he could add a bunch of fat loss offerings, but that's not what he loves doing. He loves the baseball market and he's already created a success he is enjoying, and I guarantee it's just going to get better from here.

And the example I love the most is Dave Gleason. Dave had a very successful in-home training business but didn't really love what he was doing.

He attended the first IYCA Summit and decided then and there that youth fitness was what he was meant to do.

So Dave and his wife Andrea became one of our first Athletic Revolution franchisees.

They're enjoying great success already, and it's getting better by the day. The atmosphere when we walked into his facility was incredible, and we could see just how happy they were with what they were doing.

To me, that's what this is all about. Forget all the *Four Hour Workweek* crap, you're going to spend a LOT of time working in your business, working on your business, and thinking about your business if you're going to be successful.

That's the case for all these guys, and I know that's the case for me. I work a LOT but it rarely feels like work. I absolutely love what I do and love the people I work with.

Not only do I wish the same for you – but Fitness Consulting Group is built on doing whatever it takes to make sure you can get there.

Because if you sift through all the B.S. some folks would have you believe about never having to really work and accept that you're going to be putting in your share of time and effort, you need to be building toward a success that you're going to enjoy and one that serves you instead of the other way around.

7 Hidden Fitness Marketing Tactics

When discussing marketing it's easy to fall back to the standby stuff like networking, public speaking, direct mail and PPC ads.

But these are not the only ways to grow your business. Here are 7 hidden fitness marketing tactics that will help you grow your business in a hurry.

1. **Have a 'Carrot'** - One of the best hidden fitness marketing tactics I know is to build "carrots" into your business. Martial arts does this with the belt system. Most MLM companies have this with different tiers you can ascend through by reaching certain performance benchmarks. We've even developed a system for this in our youth fitness franchise Athletic Revolution. The easiest way to build a carrot into your business is to run transformation contests so your clients have a short term deadline to shoot for. But don't limit yourself to this. There are plenty of other ways that you can set intermediate goals for your clients so they can reach certain benchmarks to reinforce their successful behavior.

2. **Recognize** - Make sure you're recognizing your clients every chance you get... the loyalty it will

build is enormous. Client of the week. Camper of the month or day. Simple acknowledgment of a job well done. An occasional card congratulating someone on their accomplishments. All of these will help you build a fiercely loyal client base that will refer people to you over and over.

3. **Social proof** - People want to see people who've been where they want to go. Collect tons of testimonials, before and after pics, and success stories. Make them a key part of every website, blog, ad, and postcard and showcase them in your facility. This will close more people for you than the best sales script ever will.

4. **Continual improvement** - If you want to keep your clients excited, continually add new features, offerings and systems. This will keep things fresh and keep your people from looking elsewhere for the "better mousetrap." Plus these new additions are great for generating publicity and to use as marketing assets.

5. **Have a Hook** - People want to feel like the person they're working with is an expert in exactly what they need. If someone wants to become a better cyclist, they want someone who is an expert in coaching cyclists. If they're moms, they want a mom's fitness expert. Figure our your hook, and it will make everything else about marketing easier.

6. **Consistently soft selling** - You should always be building value in your other offerings. If you sell supplements – talk about the benefits, share success stories, and present it as a solution when

the opportunity presents itself. You can do this without ever hard selling someone. You're just sharing solutions and successes.

7. **Over Delivering** - It goes without saying, but every day you have the opportunity to keep your clients excited about you and your business, so make sure that you do. You are delivering so much more than just results. You're delivering an experience.

Make sure the atmosphere is energetic and motivating. If you train in groups be sure to give everyone some personal attention. Send personal cards & emails. Make personal calls. Set yourself apart from every other business your clients interact with. You're guaranteed growth if you do.

So there are 7 hidden fitness marketing tactics that get overlooked more than they should.

The Hierarchy Of Client Getting

If you needed to generate new business now, what would you do?

I don't mean new clients next week or next month. I mean you need new clients NOW to pay the bills.

Would you sit at home and submit articles and press releases, or would you make blog posts and phone calls?

There are dozens of things you could do if you had to generate new clients, but which ones would pay off fastest?

With that in mind I created a simple **Hierarchy of Client Getting** activities to get you started.

Level One Activities – If you need new clients TODAY, these should be the focal point of your marketing efforts.

- Talking to members of your network face to face

- Doing public speaking

- Meeting new people through networking events and personal networking activities

- Visiting local businesses and marketing to employees or creating JV's

- Asking for referrals

As you probably noticed, these all involve face-to-face contact.

Level Two Activities – These activities are almost as effective as level one activities, however they are a little less effective, as nothing is as powerful as "belly to belly" marketing.

- Personally calling members of your network

- Making business-to-business calls

- Sending press releases to the local media

- Personally e-mailing members of your network

- Asking for referrals via mailings to your clients

- Doing reactivation calls

Why are these not as effective as level one activities? First off, a significant percentage of the time your phone calls will end up as voicemails, and your messages and emails will get lost in the volume of other calls and emails the recipient receives. Secondly – it's much harder to say 'no' in person.

Level Three Activities - These activities are valuable, but often take a while to pay off or need to be done in volume to yield big results. However, once they hit critical mass they can drive a business.

- Submitting SEO Press Releases

- Submitting articles

- Blogging
- Doing direct mailings to your network
- Sending an email newsletter
- Doing reactivation mailings
- Lead bowls or boxes
- Craigslist ads
- Facebook groups & fan pages
- Door hangers

These are all great activities that are low cost and potentially can have a huge impact on your business, but if you're running a bootcamp with 5 campers and are looking to reach 25 campers within the next 30 days – it's unlikely that these activities will get you there.

If you can outsource these and ramp them up fast that will almost always be the best approach you can take because you can focus on levels 1 & 2 but not miss out on the benefits of level 3.

Level Four Activities – Only do these activities after you've really worked the first three levels.

- Newspaper ads
- Radio ads
- Direct mail to cold lists
- Billboards
- TV ads

These can be effective – in fact we've used them all for our businesses at one time or another, but they're expensive and not going to provide you with your best ROI.

So are you getting the idea yet?

When we have coaching clients that aren't generating enough new business, 98% of the time it's because they've gotten comfortable working on level three activities and ignoring the level one and two activities.

Let me try to drive this home with an analogy for you:

If you needed someone to lend you $1000, which would you do:

A. Post a request on your blog?

B. Send someone an email to ask?

C. Send someone a letter to ask?

D. Call them and personally ask?

E. Visit them face to face and ask?

OK – that's not a perfect analogy – but you get the picture. The most powerful way to persuade someone is to do it in person or as close to in person as you possibly can.

So spend 30 minutes evaluating what percentage of your marketing time is spent on level one and level two activities. Then make an effort to increase it by at least 50%.

Three Things You Need To Have A Successful Personal Training Business

Nick and I, along with Brian Grasso and Sara Nylander, launched a youth fitness & athletic development franchise called Athletic Revolution.

We've been very deliberate with our expansion because we are committed to building the premier youth fitness & athletic development franchise in the world – and we can't do that haphazardly.

Because we spend a lot of time focusing on building Athletic Revolution the right way, we put a lot of thought into what goes into a successful fitness business. While I can't share the details of everything we've uncovered as some of it is proprietary and exclusive to AR franchisees – I can share the key components that go into any successful fitness business.

To build a successful business, you need:

A training system – If you don't have a training system you're not going to be able to build and maintain a successful business. Ever wonder why no one else talks about that? I do. If you don't have a training system for your business, it is kind of like marketing the heck out of a restaurant... without caring if the food sucks.

Operational systems – No operational systems mean that you'd better plan on running your camp or facility until you're 80.

No vacations, no sick days – no expansion.

If you want to ever grow beyond trading time for dollars – operational systems are a must.

Marketing & Sales Systems – This is the one that gets the most attention from everyone else, but without the other two – it can't create a successful business.

But if you have the foundation of the other two in place – the right marketing and sales systems are what propel you to a 6 or 7 figure business.

Honestly, most people don't do things that way.

Lots of sizzle – not so much steak.

Heck, we had to fire some "advisors" of ours because they were entirely focused on #3.

To heck with #1 and #2.

But I promise you... if you slight training and operations you'll be looking for the next fad or new get rich scheme before long while the trainers that mastered the trifecta will be thriving.

12 Common Fitness Business Mistakes You Don't Want To Make

There are a lot of mistakes personal trainers and coaches make that hold them back from reaching their business goals. Here are 12 of the most common:

Mistake #1 – Thinking that aggressive marketing will make up for a mediocre service. The bottom line is this: you can generate a lot of leads with a strong marketing push, but you won't keep those clients if you're all sizzle and no steak. You have to deliver great results, and you have to create an environment that your clients love being in.

I don't know of any great personal training business that don't get a lot of their clients from referrals. Obviously, you can't generate referrals with a run of the mill service.

Mistake #2 – Thinking that blogging, you tube videos and article writing are the best way to grow an offline business. A little while back on Personal Trainer U. a member posted complaining that he didn't have any clients. The economy was bad, the people in his town didn't have any money, and this was a bad time to be a trainer. I asked what he was doing to grow his business. He said he was submitting articles and press releases online, he was blogging 2-3 times per week, and he was really putting himself out there.

I kindly reminded him that there were probably no prospects hanging out in his home office, and he needed to get out and actually meet people in the flesh. He didn't like that answer – but most people who are unwilling to do the work don't appreciate the truth.

Look, I'm all for blogging, SEO, and You Tube – but to this day I've never seen a personal training business exclusively built from this stuff. The people who do it right blend this with high return stuff like public speaking, networking, and even direct mail – they don't think they'll just start writing a few posts and get rich.

Mistake #3 – Being a bill collector. Why did you become a trainer or a coach? To chase people around month after month reminding them to bring their check next session? Didn't think so. Do yourself a favor: set all your clients up on EFT billing, and eliminate your role as a collection agent.

Mistake #4 – Ignoring atmosphere. Atmosphere is a big part of any business's success. People want an experience. When it comes to fitness, they want energy. They want motivation. Should I also mention that a great atmosphere will generate better results? If you want people to rave about your business – to spread the word to everyone they know – atmosphere will be a key to making that happen. So when you're developing a facility, creating a camp, or planning your sessions – be sure to factor in atmosphere.

Mistake #5 – Focusing on Craigslist advertising. I like Craigslist. You know why? Because you can find stuff there – cheap. Isn't that the main reason people use Craigslist?

Besides, if something is easy to do and is free it will almost always get watered down in a hurry. That's why public speaking will always work. Sure – it's free to do but most people are scared to death of speaking in front of groups and too lazy to get speaking engagements.

So – just like some of the other stuff online I talked about in Mistake #2, I'm not saying Craigslist ads are worthless. If you're in a market that isn't already saturated – they certainly have some value – but they aren't the magic bullet for adding a bunch more clients.

Mistake #6 – Trying a dozen things to get clients and doing them all "half-assed". The most successful students we have typically use 2-3 core lead generation strategies and work them month after month. Sure, they test other strategies to see if any others really take off – but they have their bread and butter ways to get clients, and they work them. They don't just try something once and discard it. Neither should you.

Mistake #7 – Having only one revenue stream. Having only one revenue stream is a disaster waiting to happen. If all you have is bootcamps and someone comes in and undercuts you on price and steals half of your clients, or maybe summer comes and a bunch of your clients go on vacation – you're in trouble. You need to diversify. Have several income streams such as corporate camps or youth programs such as Athletic Revolution. Sell supplements. Offer camps, semi-private training, and even infoproducts.

Just don't be stuck with a single means of generating revenue.

Mistake #8 – Not knowing who you are and who you serve. Some people are better suited to run semi-private or small group programs and should pass on running bootcamps. Others aren't cut out to run kids programs.

You need to figure out what's right for you.

Decide who you love working with – those clients whose sessions you can't wait to start – 99% of the time, that's who you're meant to serve. Focus your business there.

Mistake #9 – Missing on the easiest lead source. Every time I meet with a group of trainers I ask where their new clients come from and the answers vary person to person a great deal – more than you'd expect. But the thing that surprises the most is how few trainers actually generate as many clients as they should from a structured referral process.

They may get some clients from word of mouth. They may get a few from occasional referral promotions. But instead of making new business from referrals a weekly occurrence – too many trainers settle for a fraction of that.

Mistake #10 – Missing the easy 2. Bootcamps have become much more common over the past couple of years. Health club chains like Anytime Fitness are growing like crazy. Competing for general fitness clients is probably tougher now than ever before.

If you want to go into far less competitive markets – youth fitness/athletic development and corporate fitness are ripe for the taking.

Don't think this means that you can't kill it training fat loss clients or choosing busy moms or another more common market to target – you absolutely can.

But if you want what I call "the low hanging fruit" – youth fitness/athletic development and corporate fitness are where you need to be.

Mistake #11 – Not moving to a space of your own when you can. If I've seen it once, I've seen it two dozen times. A trainer builds up a great business using someone else's space and out of nowhere the rug gets pulled out from under him/her.

Either the business they're renting space from gets greedy and wants more rent, or if it's a fitness facility, the owners decide to try to run a similar program thinking they'll make more money.

If the trainer is at a park, a competitor moves in and starts using the same location, and in doing so creates an uncomfortable environment.

So use someone else's space to build up your business – but for security, control of your own situation, and the ability to add multiple streams of income, move to your own low overhead space when you can.

Mistake #12 – Letting everyone catch up. If you're the best at something in your market – do everything you can to hold that position. It's a lot like getting a lead in sports – you want to keep your foot on the opponent's neck and lock up the victory.

But what usually happens is that the person with the initial foothold as the market leader gets lazy, loses focus, or tries too hard to expand into unrelated areas, soon losing the lead when the competitors step up their games.

Personal Training Business
Success Made Easy

I recall a phone conversation with one of our best students where he was talking about several things that he wanted to work on for his business.

Honestly, he sounded overwhelmed.

Now this isn't some guy just trying to get a business off the ground – his business had gone from zero to over $25,000 every month (more than $30,000 in some months) in less than 18 months.

But still – he sounded like a guy that was beaten down, and really it all boiled down to this: he wanted to improve about 6 or 7 things in his business, and he wanted to do them all immediately.

The word **perfectionist** came to mind.

So I'll share with you, as I did with him, a simple exercise that Nick and I used to do religiously.

At one stage in our business life we essentially had 3 business components:

1. Our personal training business & smoothie bar in Elizabethtown.

2. Our health club in Owensboro.

3. Our online based business that consisted of some coaching and products.

On Monday we'd meet for 15 minutes and pick one component of our businesses in Elizabethtown to improve during the next week.

On Wednesday we'd pick one component of our health club to improve.

Of Friday we'd pick one specific thing to improve about our online business.

The next week we'd pick something else for each.

Pretty simple, huh?

One week we might change our price presentation.

The next it might be our upsell script.

Another week it could be how we did our assessments.

Or it might be something as simple as adding an autoresponder sequence for new members or clients. But every week we did something.

Now we obviously had to keep working IN each of these businesses – and we often sought ways to improve each of them outside the meeting…

…but that simple little meeting and commitment to improving one aspect of our business each week worked wonders.

Think about it – over the course of a year that's 52 business improvements.

Little things add up.

So when I was talking with this gentleman, I told him to pick one item each week and fix it.

Let the others things he wanted to worry about just remain how they were and see one all the way through to his satisfaction each week.

Because I didn't want him to do what we all too often do when we have a number of things to do – get paralyzed not knowing where to start.

Just pick one thing and get it done.

Next week do another.

I fully expect him to have his business running like clockwork and bringing in $50,000 a month in no time using this approach – and I know it will work just as well for you.

So do yourself a favor and identify the one thing you're going to improve this week, and get to it.

Understanding The Difference
Between Activity and Achievement

If you're like most trainers or coaches – between training clients and managing your business you are likely working 50, 60, or maybe even 70 hours a week or more.

The problem with most fitness professionals is not a lack of willingness to put in long hours and work hard.

It's the way they are spending their time.

Most fitness pros are training clients for the bulk of their work day – which is totally fine. But they are also the bookkeeper, janitor (if they own a facility), marketer, and veritable jack-of-all-trades when it comes to running their business. So let's put some math to the way most trainers spend their time.

If I ask most trainers or coaches what they earn per hour the typical answer is $50-75 per hour. Unfortunately, this is usually not the case.

Where as these trainers may charge $75 per hour for their training sessions, their work day looks more like this:

Training Sessions – 4 hours per day.

Busy work/"Putting out fires" – 3 hours per day.

Wasted time surfing the 'net or doing other low return on investment activities – 2 hours per day.

Sales or marketing related activities, program design, or doing retention activities – 1 hour per day.

So this fitness pro is "on the job" for 10 hours per day and makes $300 for the day's work.

Looks to me like that trainer makes $30 per hour – not $75.

Hey, $300 a day is nothing to sneeze at. Five days per week of that is $75,000 per year. That would put you in the top 15% of all earners in the U.S.

But two things come to mind when I see that fact:

1. Most trainers don't make $75,000 per year. In fact the U.S. average is under $30,000.

2. If you truly can command $75 per hour or more for your time, why aren't you replacing some of those low return activities with more $75 per hour activities?

So think about your goals.

What is the ratio of time that you spend moving closer to your goals vs. time you spend that doesn't move you toward them or moves you away from them?

What are you doing to improve that ratio?

Personally, I am frustrated if I go a couple of hours without taking actions (even small ones) that move me closer to my goals, but I know dozens of people who go weeks – sometimes months – without taking even a step toward where they want to be.

Where do you fit into that continuum?

Your goal should be to gradually move toward spending more – and eventually most – of your time on your high return activities and delegating, streamlining, or simply eliminating your low return activities. Think about it... if you spend an hour mowing your lawn, which you could delegate to a neighborhood kid for $10 per hour, and replace that activity with a $75 per hour activity... that's a net gain of $65 per week or $260 per month. You'll soon discover that you can do that with a bunch of your activities.

Bookkeeping, website maintenance, cleaning, etc. You can find someone who doesn't place the same dollar value on their time that you do and delegate that task to them, and then replace that activity with high return activities.

So I have an assignment for you:

Choose at least one item that you can either delegate, streamline, or eliminate from your weekly task list. Act on this item. In a week, choose one more item, and continue to do so week after week until you've significantly increased the value of your time.

The Contrarian Fitness Business

I want to give you a great tip I picked up at the Dan Kennedy Super Conference from Dan Kennedy himself.

He said, "Most times you can jump to the top of any industry simply by doing everything the opposite of your competition."

I think back to launching our personal training business and only selling training in 30 minute sessions and on 12 month contracts when everyone else did hour sessions and short term packages.

Starbucks approached selling coffee from as opposite a perspective as could be.

Southwest airlines focused on getting people from one place to another on time for a low price – something unheard of in the airline industry.

If you want to be successful, look at what all the other trainers and clubs are doing – then do the opposite. If they're all selling 1 hour, one-on-one sessions, then you should do 30 minute sessions, small group training or bootcamps.

They sell in 12 and 24 packs.

You do 6 and 12 month agreements.

They try to be all things to all people.

You niche your business.

They deliver mediocre service.

You treat clients like royalty.

If you have time today, go do one of my favorite things:

"Shop" a health club.

See what they do. How they sell. What they offer.

After you see how impersonal they are and how they treat their members – go do the opposite.

You'll be on your way to building a great business.

Fitness Business Success: 3 by 11

If you want to grow your fitness business, you must spend some time working ON it along with all the time you spend working IN it.

A lot of this boils down to time management, but it's not only about saving time...

...it's about making your time more valuable.

The way you make your time more valuable is to make sure you're getting high return activities done instead of always pushing them back to spend your time "putting out fires" or just working IN your business.

Here's a simple way that you can ensure that you are spending time working ON your business every day:

Use the 3 by 11 Method.

Step One: Each evening before you go to bed, list out 3 high return activities you can accomplish the next day. These are work ON your business tasks.

Step Two: In the morning choose one of the high return activities and complete it. See it through beginning to end. If it's not something that fits into an hour or at most two – break it down into smaller components and finish one of those.

After you finish the task, check it off and move to the next one.

The goal is to finish 3 high return tasks by 11 a.m.

Step Three: Evaluate what you got done at the end of the day and create your 3 by 11 list for tomorrow.

Now you may be thinking to yourself – "Yeah, right. I'm booked solid from 5:30 –Noon almost every day."

No sweat. Pick any 3 hour window throughout the day and use that as your "by 11" time.

During that time, shut off the distractions – for me that would be random calls, ESPN, and random email – and get the things done that will take your business to the next level.

So what do you think? Is this simple enough that you can put it into action?

Making Your Fitness
Business Viral In Four Steps

Step One: Your Marketing Message – Your "message" is what you communicate to your existing and future clients, and this can sometimes have an impact on what your clients say about you. The areas to improve in your message are your *brand*, your *sales and marketing materials*, and your *values*.

Your Brand

Your brand is your company identity in the eyes of your clients. Branding is a big topic, so for now, it's important to know that you can and should improve your brand. However, once you have a good brand message, you should stick to it. If you change all the time, the "branding effect" will be greatly reduced.

Further, make sure that all your marketing materials include your brand – as it will become your business identity and will be what is conveyed when people spread the word about you.

So what is your brand?

Your Sales and Marketing Materials

Your sales and marketing materials include any form of communication that your clients or potential clients may see. You're thinking business cards and websites, but this also includes sales scripts, t-shirts, lead boxes, and anything else that spreads the word about you.

While getting "viral" is bigger than your sales materials, at some point your potential client, even if driven by word of mouth, will come in contact with these materials. The more "right" you get these materials the better, of course.

Continually improve the effectiveness of these messages by focusing on the changes that are the easiest and/or have the most impact.

Your Values

Your "values" are what you stand for as a business. I mean, what you *really* stand for. There are a great many fitness businesses that profess that they stand for a great number of noble things, but their actions prove otherwise. Whatever your values are, they will most definitely be communicated to your clients either intentionally or unintentionally. In fact, the unintentional communication, that is, the kind of communication that occurs by just being who you are, is perhaps the most significant. So what are your values?

Step Two: Quality of Service – At its core, this is what your business is. You exchange your training for your clients' money. The greater the value you give to your clients in exchange for what they give you, the more likely they are to be delighted, and that delight translates into your business going viral. But that's only part of the picture.

Giving someone high value for their dollar is a great start, but may not be enough to get people to talk about you. To do that, you need to be so excellent that you are buzzworthy, or, to put it simply, worth talking about.

Go beyond what they ask for when they become a client.

Be something so amazingly great that people will slap themselves and say. "Wow!"

Have you ever done business with someone that was "so damn good" you had to tell someone about it?

You should continually strive to improve, but remember there are times you need to stop making big changes and focus on small tweaks that most people won't notice. At that point your services will have become such an integral part of your message that they should not be publicly changed.

Constantly improve your training knowledge and the quality of your programming, but remember that clients also want a consistent experience – especially if it works.

Step Three: Client Experience

Some businesses make themselves buzzworthy with just the power of the client experience they provide. Domino's Pizza, for example, did this by being the fastest pizza delivery in the world. Not great pizza – but that wasn't their brand.

If you are excellent in both your quality of service and client experience, you are well on your way to going viral.

Here are some ways you should be constantly improving your client experience:

1. Shorten Your Client's Path Between Their Problems and Solutions – Get them results faster than everyone else.

2. Make the Process of Doing Business with You as Easy as Possible – Use EFT, answer the phone quickly, reply to emails in a timely fashion, and treat people the way you'd want to be treated.

3. Treat Your Clients with Respect – Respect their time, their effort, and everything else about them. Remember that they trusted you in what is typically an insecure time for them.

4. Make it More Than a Workout – They can get workouts at Curves, Bally's, and any number of other places. You need to provide atmosphere, energy, motivation and a genuine sense of caring.

Step Four: Referrals

Referrals can be broken down into two categories:

- Incentivized

- Inspired

Inspired referrals are the viral payoff we're discussing here– the kind that comes from giving your client an extraordinary experience. Incentivized referrals come from JV's, contests, rewards, etc. Inspired referrals will come by addressing the other 3 viral key areas of improvement. In fact, a great business that excels at those three areas alone can build a great client base founded on going viral.

Incentivized referrals, however, give your business a great boost too, especially as you're still positioning yourself as the expert in your community at a very low cost. But in general, you can't expect to build a business solely from incentivized referrals.

Unfortunately, most of the talk about referral marketing only focuses on incentivized referrals and the short-lived fireworks they can provide. Don't get caught up in the hype and think that those alone will carry you.

So remember, focus on your message, extraordinary service, and the client experience. Once you are in a process of gradually improving those things, then add in incentivized referral programs in any of the following ways:

1. Point of Sale Referrals

2. Contests

3. Rewards

4. Gift Certificates / Gift Cards

5. Bring-a-Friend

Just remember that when you "bribe" your clients (let's be honest, that's what you're doing here), you can create a rather unsavory dynamic between your clients and their friends. Take care with how you do this. Most people do this in a sort of "pitchy" way. That is to be avoided. Try to make these programs fun – and try not to make the client feel pressured.

So that's it – follow these 4 steps and start taking your business viral!

Do You Know What You Want?

I wonder if most fitness professionals really know what they want.

Dan Kennedy talks about being certain that you don't create a success that you hate.

Do you know what you want?

When I first began coaching baseball I dreamed of winning 30 games in a season and earning $30,000 a year. Considering that the team I was taking over had never won more than 19 games in a season and that the job paid $3000, those seemed like success to me.

We eventually won as many as 48 games in a season and averaged well over 30 wins for my time as a coach. During my last couple years I even earned a bit more than $30,000.

But what I never considered was that being a small college baseball coach meant more time fundraising than on baseball fundamentals and hundreds of hours riding on vans and eating at McDonalds because our budget didn't allow for anything else.

And I never considered that being a college baseball coach meant being the worst kind of employee – the kind that works for someone that doesn't have a clue what he's doing.

I recall during my final year as a coach thinking that if the job that I had was vacant, I'd not even consider applying.

And to think that being a college baseball coach was my "dream job."

After I left coaching and moved into the fitness industry, initially I thought that I'd love to own my own studio or maybe even a few. But over time I found that training clients for fat loss did not give me the same thrill that training athletes had provided.

I did find that I loved the business side of fitness and for quite some time thought that Nick and I would open a chain of gyms throughout our region.

We pursued this for a while, with a training company in one town and a gym 90 minutes away. We looked at real estate, met with investors, and even worked with a franchisor about securing the rights to all of Kentucky. As time passed, however, a few things happened:

- We realized that having to borrow enough money to open the gyms would leave us without a significant profit for quite a while.

- Dealing with developers and investors left some of our decisions and potential for success in others' hands.

- Running back and forth between Elizabethtown and Owensboro 2-3 times per week wasn't allowing me to enjoy time with my family.

- We recognized that finding, training and managing employees is a battle that is ongoing and dozens of gyms meant hundreds of employees.

None of these things were the type of success that I wanted.

During this same period, we started to do business coaching and consulting and began to offer products to fitness professionals.

Not too long after, we acquired ownership in the IYCA.

Things started to feel right.

I can't say that I love doing products; I much prefer coaching programs, live events, and Mastermind Groups. Products are a necessary and valuable component of what we do, but I love interacting with people.

Now we're co-owners in over a dozen businesses, and I'm happier than I've ever been.

- I get to coach motivated people in something I've grown to be very passionate about…business.

- I get to work in the areas of our businesses that I'm best suited to work.

- I'm home most of the time. Sure, I travel some, but I'm home more than 95% of the people I know, and I work from home 90% of the time.

- I've come full circle and get to work in athletic development through the IYCA, Athletic Revolution, and several other projects– the area of this industry that attracted me in the first place.

- My wife Holly works at home as well, and I get to play a part in helping her do what she loves.

- We've launched a franchise that I truly believe will span the globe, help hundreds of fitness professionals realize their career dreams, and help hundreds of thousands of young people.

So I finally have a pretty good idea of what I want.

- I want to be home more often than not so I can enjoy time with Holly & Tyler.

- I want to work primarily with entrepreneurs.

- I want to focus on business development and athletic development. I could spend all day in these areas and never feel like it's been work.

- I want to coach or partner with like-minded entrepreneurs to help them achieve their goals.

- I want to personally own at least one facility as I never want to be just a "theory" guy.

- I want to leave a legacy and create something that lives on.

Oh, and I want a beach house.

I'm not telling you all this because I think you need to be anything like me. Far from it. The things that Holly wants in her career are different than mine.

The key is discovering what you want your success to look like. It's been a slow process for me and it continues to evolve day by day, but I love what I'm doing now, and financially things have never been better for me or our businesses in spite of the economic issues we've heard so much about.

So think about what parts of your career/business that you love.

Think about the parts you don't.

Think about what's important to you.

Think about where you want to be a year from now... or even 3, 5, or 10 years from now.

Then start moving that direction.

It's not an overnight process. If you want more freedom, start creating systems and hiring help.

If you want to own a facility, start saving some money, writing a business plan, and looking at locations.

If you want to train only athletes, at least start by training one athlete.

But you can think bigger than that if you want.

If you want to become a famous speaker, start speaking to someone... anyone. If you want to write a book, start with a sentence. If you want to move, follow the big green signs that will direct you out of town...

Because I believe that it's never a finished product. Your wants will always be changing, and so will your circumstances, but if you're moving in the direction you want, I suspect you'll be pretty happy. And you may get farther than you ever expected.

Fitness Marketing: You
Don't Have To Do Everything

The following is a story from my time in Dallas at the Dan Kennedy Super Conference.

On Saturday morning of the conference, I got to spend some time with King Hoover.

King is a long time customer and friend that has been part of our original Trainer's Inner Circle program and is currently a Bootcamp Blueprint & IYCA member. He's also one of the most humble and kind gentlemen I've met.

King started our conversation almost apologetically, saying that he was a little upset with himself for not implementing all the great marketing strategies we've provided in the Blueprint.

I had to laugh a little.

King's built a great business in Fort Worth, Texas and he's had his own syndicated radio show, is on TV and is about as media friendly as can be.

And he's probably the best networker I know.

By the time I sat down with King for breakfast he'd already befriended the guy at the next table and knew all about his business. He also treated our server like she was a Head of State.

King treats EVERYONE that way.

No hidden agenda.

No "what can this person do for me" attitude.

He just treats everyone like we all want to be treated – and like we all should treat people.

In every interaction without exception.

And that's his go to marketing strategy... being an outgoing, friendly, and good person.

In fact, a while back King helped a gentleman lose some weight.

This man happened to be a security guard... not a CEO or the President of a big company.

As with everyone King interacts with, this man saw how genuine King was and how much he cared about his clients.

Over the years they've stayed in touch and recently King received a call from this now former security guard.

The man now sees over some community based programs with the Texas Rangers baseball team and has invited King to run fitness camps and programs for kids (as I mentioned, King's an IYCA member), families, and adults.

King gets to use the Rangers stadium, gets his signage around the park, and is essentially partnering with a Major League Baseball team (that draws 2 million fans a year) to be their preferred fitness provider.

And it all started with King just building a relationship.

I'm not suggesting that you should drop everything you're doing and just focus on networking since that's the foundation of King's marketing efforts.

That's his strong suit.

If it's yours too, maybe you should ramp up your efforts there a bit.

But if not, pick 1 or 2 things that can be your go to marketing strategies and work them to no end.

King's built his business with networking.

It's better to be great at a couple strategies than mediocre at a bunch.

And King's living proof that you never know what doors might open if you just keep knocking.

Marketing Without Spending a Fortune

One of the most common questions I get goes something like this:

"How can I fill up my schedule without spending a fortune on ineffective advertising or direct mail?"

What they really mean is:

I don't have enough clients. Can you help?

Well, the better question is, "What didn't I do in the past few weeks to cause me not to have as many clients as I want?" I guess what I'm saying is the answer lies in *your own actions.* Every day you get to decide whether you're going to work on your business or just complain about the problems within your business.

So, with that in mind, here are several things you can do ASAP to get things rolling... if you're willing to take ACTION:

1. Evaluate your sales system

Without an effective sales system, an increase in leads isn't going to help you much. You need to have a systematic approach for presenting your offerings to your prospects that will give you the highest possible outcome when it comes to generating clients and increasing revenue. Here are some tips:

- Use a script. Every presentation should be the same. Develop your best approach, and use it every time.

- Use an alternate choice close. Present 2-3 options and ask the prospect which one they want to get started with.

- If your ideal offering is a 3 session per week bootcamp, make sure there is a 4 or 5 session per week option. This will make the 3 session per week option look less expensive by comparison.

Bottom line: bad sales system = bad income.

2. An easy way to ask for referrals

While you should have several referral systems in place, this one is probably the easiest. EVERY time someone says anything positive about your services reply with this:

"I'm so glad you're seeing great results and enjoy working with me. I enjoy working with people like you that are truly motivated to achieve their goals. (Pause) By the way, most of our new clients are referrals from current clients that are enjoying their experience with us – so if you're pleased with your progress please tell your friends that would like to achieve similar results about us."

Many will respond by saying that they've already told someone about you. If that is the case, then simply thank them for doing so by providing them with a gift card or certificate that they can provide to a referral.

3. An easy way to reactivate former clients

Here is a simple way to reactivate former clients. Go though your database, and call your former clients using this simple script:

"Hi _____, this is _____ from XYZ Personal Training. I just wanted to give you a call to see how you've been doing since your last camp/session?"

If they say they're doing fine, simply say:

"I am so glad to hear that. If you need anything or want to come back in for a session, please give me a call."

If the response is something like, *"I've been slacking on my workouts,"* or, *"I need to get back on track,"* follow up with:

"Let's schedule you to come back in for a free session this week. Which is better for you, Tuesday or Wednesday?"

Remember, if people forget about you they can't refer.

4. Reaching out to local businesses

If you want to fill up your bootcamp with prospects fast, you can do a business call campaign. A business call campaign is probably not in everyone's comfort zone, but if you're willing to do it you are guaranteed to generate a bunch of new prospects in a hurry. The added benefit to something like this is that it makes your camp a lot more energetic with bigger numbers and really expands your network in a hurry. So here is what you do.

Pull out the phone book and turn to the yellow pages. Start with the 'A's' and begin calling all local businesses that might have an employee that fits your target market. Here is a easy script for you to use:

*" Hello, this is _____ from _____ and in celebration of our "Get (Your City) Fit Month" I wanted to call a few local businesses, and the **first person to answer the phone WINS A FREE TWO WEEK COMPLIMENTRAY MEMBERSHIP to my** fitness bootcamp...........*

AND THAT'S YOU!!!!!

CONGRATULATIONS!!!!!

*Now all you have to do is RSVP by going to my website and entering your claim number in the next 48 hours (have form or contact page) or by coming to camp orientation this Saturday at 10 a.m. to secure your spot in this month's camp......**Would you rather attend orientation this SATURDAY or register through the website and attend the orientation next week??? GREAT!!!!** And your first and last name was? And I also need second phone number where you can be reached?*

*Ok _____, when you come to orientation, ask for **(name)** and it should take about 10 minutes to get you registered. And if for some reason you cannot make your appointment (**DATE/TIME**) – can we count on you to give us a call back at (number) with a better time?"*

If you commit to making a dozen calls a day you'll get 3-4 people that want to take you up on your offer. Of those, 1-2 will show up to camp. Five days a week of that means 5-10 new leads a week, or 20-40 new leads per month.

Now, here's how you turn them into paying clients:

Following orientation or the first day of camp, show them that they can trade in the 2 weeks for one month free if they enroll in the next camp (or 2 camps... your choice) if they choose to during their first visit.

Even if you only convert 25%, that's 5-10 new campers per month. Not bad for a few phone calls.

So there you have it, four ways to add more prospects and more clients without spending a dime. And remember, these are in addition to the things you should be doing on a daily and weekly basis while executing your fitness business growth plan. If you're working a plan list, you should have no problem filling up your schedule in a hurry, with almost zero out of pocket cost.

What Are You Missing?

In golf, they talk about fixing one aspect of your game and shaving a handful of strokes off your score all at once. If you get better at putting, all of a sudden those 90's that you're shooting become 85's. If you get better at pitching and chipping those 85's become 80's.

I think that same approach will work for improving your business numbers too. I'm going to use bootcamps as my example, but this approach works for any fitness business. Here are some areas for improvement and some simple steps to make that happen.

The Quality of Your Camps– If your camps are bad, there is no amount of marketing that will mask it. You should be retaining *at least* 80% of your people from one month to the next. If you're not, something about the way you're delivering your camp is broken. Here are some tips to fix it:

- Implement the Workout Muse system. It's a proven, done-for-you system that will not only give you a complete format to follow for your camps, but it will also add energy to each session.

- Plan ahead. If you're thinking up your camp workout 15 minutes before camp... stop! These people are paying you to help them achieve their goals, so you should be prepared.

- Be complete. While you can't individually design each campers program, you can certainly make sure that each session combines all the elements of a well designed training session. Group training shouldn't mean bad training.

- Bring it. Every day you have to bring energy, personality, enthusiasm and be ready to motivate and inspire. Your camps should be a high point in each of your campers' days. If they're not, your business will struggle.

A Consistent Approach To Marketing– If you have low numbers, you have to assume that means you aren't marketing. Every day you should be doing things to generate new prospects. Here are the marketing strategies I'd focus on:

- Public speaking. If you're not doing at least 2 speaking engagements per month you're leaving money on the table. If my numbers were low, I'd be doing one speaking engagement per week.

- Networking. Nothing sexy about it, but you should be passing out 2 week trials – preferably 3 every day – attending networking events weekly, and reaching out to everyone already in your personal network.

- Business of the Week. This has been a winner for the Bootcamp Blueprint members. You should be contacting 2-4 businesses per week at minimum.

- The fundraiser. This was a Bootcamp Blueprint exclusive that was a killer. Great for business growth and great for your community. A win-win for sure. Just identify an organization that needs to raise money, and reach out to that organization with your fundraising opportunity. They keep all the proceeds, and you get all the leads.

Work those four and work them hard. Your numbers are guaranteed to climb.

Converting Prospects To Clients & Referrers– Every prospect should be considered precious when you're trying to grow your business. Here's how to get them to buy and refer more often:

- Personal attention. A personal call to each prospect. A personal introductory session. A card thanking them for coming to camp. People want to be treated well and feel important. Provide that and they'll not only become clients... they'll become raving fans.

- A scripted offer. If you don't have a scripted sales presentation, then you're missing sales, plain and simple. I've provided a script in several different venues... Boot Camp Blueprint, my free Fitness Sales e-book, and Personal Trainer U... model this script, and close more deals. If you're getting most of your prospects in on free trials, offer to allow them to "trade in" their trial for a big discount for the next month or 3 month program.

- Ask for referrals early. As soon as someone joins camp, even on a trial, ask for referrals. Ask them to give you the names and contact information of 3-5 people that they might like to join them in camp so that you can provide them with 2 week free trials. If a referral joins, you'll give the referrer $50 off the next month.

Making It Easy To Stay – You need to make it easy to continue to work with you. Sounds simple, but it's amazing how many trainers make doing business with them difficult. Here are some tips:

- Be easy to pay. Implement auto-renewal. Use automated billing software, and set up your business so you're not chasing money at the beginning of each month. With auto-renewal, the responsibility to stop working with you is now on the client instead of the burden of re-signing people falling to you. This simple step will improve retention 25% for sure.

- Move people to 3 month or longer commitments. From this point forward, start selling 3 month contracts to all new prospects. Don't get caught up in moving your current campers to anything beyond auto-renewal, but have all new people make 3 month commitments.

- Have a downsell. If someone can't continue at 3, 4, or 5 sessions per week, offer to downgrade their program to 2 sessions per week.

There are certain areas in everyone's business that, if improved, will provide a big surge in business. Identify those areas – start with my suggestions above – and start growing your business today!

3 Things Coaching College Baseball Taught Me About Business

A while ago, I traveled to Portsmouth, Ohio, to visit the University where I used to coach. They were honoring the team I coached that finished 5th at the World Series, so I got to see some of my former players and throw out the first pitch for their game. It was fun.

Well, I've said this a number of times before, but coaching taught me a lot. Because we were a program with pretty limited resources, I had to learn how to achieve success by doing some things differently than the competition since we weren't going to compete by having more scholarships (we had about 1/10 the number our best competitors had) or a nicer facility (we used a city owned park).

So I read books on business and marketing as well as the typical coaching fare – looking for an advantage. Here are three strategies that I used that allowed us to become a nationally competitive program despite having resources that were better suited for a high school team that can be utilized to achieve similar success in business.

Find Opportunity Where Others Don't – In baseball, coaches typically allocate a lot of their scholarship money for pitchers and shortstops. They invest a lot of practice time on things like pickoff plays and obscure bunt defenses.

Not me.

We weren't going to outspend our competition for the pitchers they wanted – so I focused my energies on aggressively going after players with great offensive potential that were undervalued by the competition and just tried to find diamonds in the rough when it came to pitchers or shortstops. When it came to practice time – instead of spending much time on things that happen 5% of the time in the game, I dedicated our practices to 2 things:

1. The things that happen most of the time in games. The basics.

2. Making our players better athletes. We took an approach to strength & conditioning similar to that of football programs while most other teams were still using Nautilus machines.

It sounds kind of obvious, but it's certainly not the norm in baseball.

Transitioning to the business world, this approach led me to gravitate toward 30 minute 1 on 1 sessions, group based training, and EFT billing.

To apply this in your own business, look at what others don't do or don't do well. If no one offers youth programs, there's your opportunity. If no one specifically targets moms, there you go. If no one has a quality service option for $99, find a way you can help people a lot at that price.

There are undervalued opportunities in EVERY business and EVERY market; it's your job to find them.

Play To Your Strengths– Once I identified a formula that worked for building our team, I just expanded on it. I worked on recruiting an even better caliber of player that fit the same mold. I kept refining the system. I didn't try to also do all the things the competitors were doing. I simply wanted to create the best possible version of our organization.

In the business world – this means don't try to be all things to all people. Pick a couple of things, and be extraordinary at them. When it comes to marketing – hone in on 2-3 core systems, and work them aggressively every day until your business is where you want.

Strive to be known as the go to expert for a couple of niche markets in your community. With a little focus, you can own those markets.

Get Personal– My biggest strength as a coach was as a recruiter, and my recruiting was simple:

1. Create a "product" players would want to be a part of.

2. Build and cultivate relationships with the players that would be a good fit for what we were trying to do.

So I made a LOT of personal calls and a lot of visits to get to know people. I went to tons of coaching clinics to build relationships with the high school coaches. I took the prospects and their families on tours when they came to campus instead of delegating it. If getting the right players was the most important factor in being successful, then getting personal was my way of doing it.

Business is the same. For our mastermind groups, you don't ever see sales copy or email promos. We want to get to know the people that are going to be in the groups to make sure they're a good fit. Personal calls are a perfect way to do that.

If you want to see an immediate uptick in your business, take every interaction you make up one level:

- If you normally send a mass email, send a personal one.

- If you normally send a personal email, make a call.

- If you normally make a call, visit in person.

I guarantee you'll love the results.

So there you have it, three lessons learned from coaching college baseball that have continued to help me time and time again in business. They've all worked well for me. Now let them work for you.

12 Months Of Fitness Referrals

Every fitness professional knows the importance of generating referrals as it relates to business growth, so why do so many struggle to implement referral programs in their businesses?

My guess is that they don't set deadlines to implement what they know. So I'm going to set some deadlines for you. Here are 12 months worth of referral generating ideas. All you have to do is follow the formula and watch your referral business grow!

Week 4 – Set up an ongoing referral program. If you don't already have one set up, you should do so immediately. There is no excuse now not to have an ongoing referral program in place. Simply come up with a reward that you will provide to clients and members of your network that send new business to you. The optimal approach is to reward the act of referring prospects to you and also reward the referring party when their referrals become clients.

Week 8 – Run a transformation challenge. Twelve weeks in length is a good starting point. This is a great referral generation machine because people will ask for help from friends and inevitably tell them what they are involved in. Don't hesitate to give away supplements as a prize.

Week 12 – Begin including a 21 day referral offer with all new client or camper purchases. Include an offer that gives them a discount on dues for each new person they refer during their first 21 days.

Week 16 – Begin a campaign of integration marketing. While this won't boost referrals per se, it will get an influx of steady new prospects into your business. Integration marketing basically is trying to integrate your offerings into other businesses' marketing and sales processes.

Week 20 – Begin sending out birthday gifts to all your clients. You can collect their birthday at the enrollment process in an unobtrusive way, letting them know that you need it to send them a birthday gift. However, this should always be optional. On their birthdays, send them a gift card or some free supplements for themselves and a friend.

Week 24 – Set up a campaign associated with the next major holiday. Tell your clients that they and a friend will get a discount on a program or product during the holiday period.

Week 28 –Send out an email or card to all your clients saying that you're doing a new client drive this week and would like to know if they have any family or friends who would be interested in doing a free trial with you. Give them some kind of gift or incentive for every person they bring in. In addition, make sure that they have a gift card that they can give to their friends or family members to entice them to do business with you. In other words, you're not just having the client tell the friend about you, the client is giving a free gift card away that will bring them back to your business.

Week 31 – Add a bring a friend function to your business. If you run camps or group training, this is easy. Just have a day or even a week each month where your clients can bring friends to their sessions.

Week 36 – Run another transformation challenge. Use what you learned from your initial challenge to make this an even bigger success.

Week 40 – Begin giving plastic gift cards to your clients. A plastic gift card with a magnetic strip on the back is a better tool than a coupon so it will set you apart from the competition. Your clients will then have the opportunity to provide these to their friends, and it will have a significant perceived value. Whenever a member of your network or a client provides someone with one of these cards this also gives them a chance to tell your story in a very unobtrusive and natural way.

Week 44 – Hold another referral contest. Incentivize your clients by giving them a cash reward or a big prize like a mini-vacation. Just think big and create a huge buzz. The possibilities are endless.

Week 48 – Conduct a one-time-only tell-a-friend offer or incentive. For example: Tell two to three friends about us, and you can get this free weight management class. The important thing to remember here is that if you said that the one-time offer is one-time only, you must stick with that. This means that next time you conduct a special offer or opportunity, your existing clients will know that when you say one-time, they'd better jump on the bandwagon now, or they'll miss out!

Week 52 –Run another transformation challenge. Use the before and afters from the first two and leverage the success of those events to pull in sponsors and publicity.

So there you have it – a full 12 month calendar to make sure you are maximizing your referral efforts. All you need to do is implement!

107 Fitness Marketing Tactics

I have brainstormed a list of all the ways that we've tried to generate clients & members in our training businesses and health club, and I figured it might be something you'd want to see. I'm not sure I have everything listed, but here's a pretty comprehensive list of 107 things we've personally used in our own businesses. Hopefully there will be a few ideas you can try...

1. **Referral Contests, Everyone Wins** – I prefer this over all other referral contests...everyone gets something for providing a referral or a lead plus are entered to win a bigger prize. One or two people take away the Grand Prize(s).

2. Referral Contest – Limited Winners

3. **Point of Sale Referral Request** – Probably my favorite lead generator. Incentivize with a t-shirt.

4. **Pay Per Referral** – We've offered $50 bills for short 3 day referral promos and it worked pretty well.

5. Gift Per Referral

6. Face To Face Referral Request

7. Letter Requesting Referral

8. Email Requesting Referral

9. Greeting Card Requesting Referral

10. Phone Call Requesting Referral

11. **Gift Per Lead For Clients & Members** – Very similar to #3, except the offer is made to all clients or members.

12. **1 Session Free Trials** – We've tested a variety of free trial offers and we've seen that the longer the trial, the more people that actually take you up on the offer. This doesn't necessarily mean that the quality of the lead for a longer trial is as good as quality for a shorter trial; it just means you'll get more prospects in front of you. If you're having trouble getting trials to show, make the trial offer stronger. If all you get are tire kickers, shorten it up.

13. 2 Session Free Trials

14. 3 Session Free Trials

15. 1 Week Free Trials

16. 2 Week Free Trials

17. 21 Day Free Trials

18. 1 Month Free Trials

19. Lead Boxes

20. Lead Bowls

21. Pay-Per-Click Ads

22. Radio Ads

23. TV Ads

24. **Flier Drops** – We've put fliers on car windshields, in newspaper bins, in teachers' school mailboxes and any number of other places. Lead boxes, door hangers, fliers and other low cost tactics require little money but a little hustle and can pay off if you're willing to do the work.

25. **Craigslist Ads** – As opposed to what some may think, I don't hate Craigslist ads. I think they can be a solid part of a marketing plan provided you remember 2 things: 1) People on Craigslist are there looking for something cheap. 2) If you think Craigslist Ads can be the centerpiece of your marketing efforts, I have a great piece of oceanfront property right here in Kentucky I'd like to sell you.

26. In Club Signage

27. **Plastic Gift Cards** – I like these better than the other gift cards and gift certificates since they have a higher perceived value.

28. Billboards

29. Magazine Ads

30. Newspaper Ads

31. **Health Fair Booths** – At all booths, your job is simple. Get contact information. That's it. You don't need to sell or even really educate on the spot; there is almost always too much going on at

the time to really build much value in what you do. Get the contact information and follow up.

32. Facebook Ads

33. Fitness Studies

34. Transformation Contests

35. **Business of the Month Offers**– This is a popular one for some of the Bootcamp Blueprint members and has sold us a couple hundred gym memberships.

36. Business of the Week Offers

37. Client Appreciation Events

38. Three Letter Sequences

39. Postcards

40. Greeting Cards

41. Invitations

42. **Business Cards** – My key to having success when handing out a business card is pretty simple... get the contact information of the recipient in return and follow up.

43. Bridal Fair Booths

44. Charity Walks

45. Charity Runs

46. Charity Contests

47. Mini-Clinics

48. Paid Clinics

49. Free Clinics

50. **Fundraiser Sales** – This is one I dreamed up after spending a decade as a coach. Find an organization that needs to raise money and let them sell short term memberships to your program or facility. Let them keep all the proceeds. You get the leads, and they raise funds.

51. **Fundraiser Clinics** – All of the clinics are geared at building a youth based business. This is a favorite of mine... offer to do a clinic for a local youth sports league and donate the proceeds to them. They have to promote it and provide the space. They raise some much needed revenue and you get a ton of qualified prospects.

52. Community Events

53. Lunch and Learns

54. Speaking to Groups

55. Speaking to Businesses / Corporations

56. Speaking to Schools / Churches

57. Brochures

58. Business to Business Calls

59. Residential Calls

60. Yard Signs

61. **"Train Them Until They Buy"**– Back when I managed about 70 trainers, I had a simple system for them to generate business is things were slow. Always be training. You should always be training someone. It can lead to them buying,

generate referrals (you can make that the stipulation for you training them), or just help you create a buzz. If you're in a club, people will most likely have more interest in working with the busy trainers – so stay busy.

62. **Radio Offers At Half Off And Keeps The Proceeds**– We've done this and had solid results with it, but our MM Group members Kevin & Kristen Harvey are the real experts on this promo and kill with it in Chattanooga.

63. Trade Outs For Leads/Referrals

64. Booths at Fairs

65. Booths at League Sign Ups

66. SEO

67. Online Local Listings

68. Endorsed Mailings

69. Endorsed Emails

70. Email Newsletters

71. Email Broadcast Offers

72. Email Autoresponders

73. Print Newsletters

74. **Low Cost Entryway Program** – Our 21 Day Drop a Dress Size program and other low risk offers like that will appeal to people your normal programs might not reach.

75. Low Cost Paid Trials

76. **Networking At Group Events** – Chamber of Commerce, BNI and all the normal group networking events are all great resources, but you should also consider expanding to other more niched groups (we had good results with the Women's Junior League among others) and online groups like MeetUp.

77. **One-on-One Networking** – Probably the most important thing you do. It can not only lead to direct sales, but also to referrals, public speaking opportunities, corporate deals, joint ventures, and pretty much anything else you might be trying to do to grow your business.

78. Wine Tasting Event

79. Radio Remote

80. **Doctor Referral** – Every month we get a couple new health club members that are referred from a local physician. It may take a bit of work to establish a relationship with a local doctor, but it's well worth the effort.

81. Corporate Discounts

82. Corporate Programs

83. **Group Special Offers**– Teacher's Appreciation Week, Administrative Professionals Week and any other day/week/month that highlights a certain group is a great excuse to make an offer specifically to them.

84. Automobile Signage

85. Gift Memberships for Silent Auctions

86. Door Hangers

87. **Door to Door Sales** – Yep, we've even sent people door to door selling 3 month gym memberships. If people can sell magazines and all-purpose cleaner, we figured we'd give it a shot, and it worked pretty well.

88. **Cross Promotions with Other Businesses** – Health food or exercise equipment stores handing out your gift cards when their customers make purchases is an easy way to get in front of good leads.

89. **Paid "Ambassadors"** – If you can find someone that is willing to promote on your behalf, give them some trial passes or gift cards and tell them that for every one that is redeemed you'll pay them $10. You can obviously up the payout if leads convert.

90. Lead From New Member Sales

91. Calls to Former Members

92. Emails to Former Members

93. Letters to Former Members

94. **Calls to Missed Sales** – We work our list of missed sales and former clients/members pretty regularly, making different offers and reaching out at the peak seasons when people are most likely to be interested (January, Fall)

95. Emails to Missed Sales

96. Letters to Missed Sales

97. Voice Broadcasts

98. Bring a Friend Events

99. Bring A Friend Periods (Week/Month)

100. Val Pak

101. Raffles

102. Gift Certificates

103. Home Association Newsletters

104. **League Sponsorships** – Probably not a big winner by itself, but if you're offering youth programs and want to build a relationship with the league, offer to do a sponsorship if they allow you to do a clinic or will email their list for you.

105. **Wall of Fame** – If you have your own space, use it for in club promotions of your ancillary offerings and to showcase your success stories. This is one of my favorite low cost marketing tools.

106. Testimonial Book

107. Payroll Stuffer

11 Ways To Explode
Your Fitness Business

We all want business growth. More clients. Different programs. A new facility. The list goes on and on.

It's just part of being a fitness entrepreneur.

Here are 11 different ways you can absolutely achieve explosive growth in your fitness business. Some, like group training, might be old news to you but can be tweaked a bit to add thousands of dollars to your bottom line. Others like warehouse facilities might be something you've given a little thought to but haven't been certain if it was right for you.

Warehouse Facilities – I think warehouse facilities are to our industry now what bootcamps used to be. They offer the best of both worlds – the opportunity to run group training and bootcamps and having your own dedicated space at a low cost.

SoI fully expect the trend of these types of gyms to really take off, and just like with bootcamps or youth training, if you're at the front of the curve, things are way easier. If you're a bootcamp owner, I'd be on the lookout for low cost space of your own. It will give your clients a destination, give you options to add revenue streams, and give you more security.

Group Training – I've said it a hundred times before, and I'll say it thousands of times more – you need to be offering group training. Bootcamps, small group, clinics, camps, semi-private... they all provide you an opportunity to better leverage your time, allow you to make more money, and also permit more people to benefit from what you have to offer due to lower per-person price points.

But here's the thing – most people are only thinking bootcamps when they think group training. Why not offer groups of 4-8 during some time slots that you couldn't necessarily fill up a bootcamp? Then you can offer more niche-specific group training like one for moms or one for combat conditioning. Whatever market you want to reach but may not have enough traction in to justify a full camp is a good place to start.

Multiple Streams of Income – If you want to thrive, you almost have to be generating revenue from more than one area. Every really successful fitness professional I know has at least 3-4 different revenue streams adding to their pool of income with many having 10 or more. I'd strongly suggest that you have a minimum of 3 revenue streams going at any time.

Hustle – I know of NO fitness professional that is enjoying business success that doesn't hustle. If you want to grow your business and your income, you MUST be willing to get on the phone, network, knock on doors, and do the things that most people don't do. While everyone else was sitting around complaining about how bad the economy was over the past few years, we have had Bootcamp Blueprint and Elite Mastermind members killing it during this time.

Tighten Up Your Niche – People want to deal with experts, so be one. Don't be a generalist. If you serve everyone, then you eliminate your best point of differentiation. If you train everyone, but the prospect is looking for help with his son who is a baseball player, will they choose you or the fitness professional who specializes in training the baseball players? Be sure to position yourself as an expert in a niche (or several niches). This will make marketing easier and allow you to price your services higher. Use the approach with smaller group training I mentioned earlier to reach a few different niche markets.

Offer Corporate Programs – A lot of fitness professionals are seeing an extraordinary amount of success by offering fitness programs/bootcamps to businesses. Some are offering full scale wellness programs while others are just making private bootcamps available to the businesses' employees. The beauty of this is that you can fill up a group program by marketing to a single business. Corporate programs are a great profit center to add to any fitness business.

Train Young Athletes – The truth is that parents will continue to spend their disposable income on their kids long after they quit spending it on themselves. This is the fastest growing segment of the fitness industry by virtually all accounts, and you'd be foolish to ignore it as a major profit center for your business.

Add in a few group offerings focused on the youth (6-18 yrs old) market, and you'll easily see an additional $2000-$4000 in monthly revenue.

Keep Studying – The successful fitness pros I know are all attending seminars, participating in coaching and mastermind groups, and reading/listening to information to improve themselves as professionals. Don't limit yourself to studying what you love. If you're weak in an area, brush up on it. This goes for training and business. I have consistently invested more than $15,000 (and sometimes significantly more than that) per year in continuing education and have always received a 10 to 1 ROI for every dollar spent.

Always Be Marketing – While most fitness pros only market when things are slow, you need to be marketing 365 days per year. That doesn't mean you have to spend an arm and a leg on advertising. Instead, focus on getting at least 4-8 low cost, high return marketing systems in place and keep testing out ways to improve them

Set Goals and Make Them Happen. Set a target and hit it. If you want 5 new clients a month, set it as your goal, and create a plan to reach it. If you want to earn $100,000 next year, you need to make $8333 a month. Find a plan that gets you there and execute it. Write down everything you want to accomplish; break it into short term goals, and then each day take small actions to accomplish them. It's not rocket science, but it's works.

Be The Anti-Health Club. 99% of health clubs don't get it. They do nothing more than rent access to equipment for their members. If you want to be successful, go to a big box gym and study everything they do... then do the opposite. Treat your clients like gold and build relationships. Focus on delivering great results and an outstanding experience. Send cards, recognize accomplishments, and treat people the way you like to be treated.

Do that along with implementing the other tips, and you'll be well on your way to a being the dominant fitness business in your market.

OK – there you have it. 11 different ways that you can see some serious business growth.

Lessons I've Learned Along The Way

When I first found out my wife was pregnant with our youngest son Alex, I was very excited. With that exciting news also came some reflection over how much has happened over the past few years.

There have been a lot of lessons along the way; here are some of the most important ones...

1. Deadlines make the difference when it comes to getting stuff done. All my biggest successes have come with deadlines attached to them.

2. My favorite times are simple family "hang outs" like when Holly, Tyler, and I watch a ballgame or movie. Nothing beats quality family time.

3. My favorite business times are our Mastermind Meetings. I love being surrounded by like-minded, entrepreneurial fitness pros.

4. It's often said that you're the average of the five people you associate with the most. Over the last few years I've certainly seen this hold true over and over.

5. There is a much stronger correlation between your practical education – stuff like Perform

Better events, business coaches, etc – and your professional success than there is a relationship between your formal education and your professional success.

6. 9 times out of 10 your biggest limiting factor is your own mind.

7. Determine what you enjoy doing and do best, and then outsource as much of the rest as possible. For me that's writing, working with coaching clients and members of our various programs, developing game plans for our businesses, and finding opportunities for growth. Those are my top areas of focus. Loading blog posts and newsletters and doing tech work are not.

8. If you want your problems solved, start looking for solutions rather than dwelling on the problems.

9. Successful people implement stuff in a hurry. The faster your speed of implementation, the bigger your bank account.

10. It doesn't matter what you know. It matters what you apply. If you don't apply something, it's wasted knowledge.

11. Focus on behaviors rather than outcomes. You can control behaviors, and by disciplining yourself to enforce new behaviors, you'll almost always assure yourself of getting the outcome you want.

12. The first couple weeks of doing something outside your comfort zone are always the hardest.

Discipline yourself to get through that, and you'll typically be able to stay the course. For me, writing was like pulling teeth in the beginning. Now it's one of my favorite things.

13. Business is like fitness. There is no magic pill, and results don't come overnight. Focus on the process, and you'll get there. Enjoy the journey.

14. The "free" line has been moved. Most successful people I know give a lot of value away.

15. Investing in yourself is better than any stock you can buy. We spent more on our business education in the past year than ever before, and our business doubled. Invest in yourself if you want to grow.

16. The most important thing I do for my business is to plan my day the evening before.

17. People will pay more money for you to make their lives easier. The more you can provide as "done-for-you" for your audience, the better off you'll be. Watch infomercials, and they'll prove this to you time and time again.

18. I've observed hundreds of fitness pros over the years, and it's as true as ever: Do the same thing you've always done, and you'll get the same thing you've always gotten. The people I've enjoyed watching that have achieved tremendous growth all stepped out of their comfort zones to get there.

19. Learn by "doing," not by talking about it. If you want to get good at public speaking... speak.

Want to get good at writing... write. Want to become a better salesperson... get in front of more people and sell.

20. It never has changed and never will: You can't help people until they want to help themselves.

21. The grass is not greener on the other side. The grass only gets greener if you water it.

22. Treat others the way you want to be treated. That's the most important business advice you'll ever receive.

23. Life isn't always fair. Accept it and move on to making the most of the hand you're dealt.

24. Luck does happen... people do get lucky. And you're a lot more likely to do so if you put yourself in the right spot for luck to happen. Even the people who win the lottery at least had bought a ticket.

25. It's never too late to start following your dreams.

26. Learn from people that have enjoyed success similar to the kind you want. Model what they've done to get where they are.

27. High achievers aren't smarter or more talented... they just do the things everyone else just dreams about doing.

Focus and Diversify:
A Recipe For Success

That doesn't make any sense does it?

Bear with me, and maybe I'll change your mind.

A great way to build a business is to dive headfirst into a niche and do everything you can to own it.

If you want to become the preeminent resource for a specific market, you need to focus your efforts there. But don't mistake focus for being a one trick pony.

My friend Jason Ferruggia is the go to guy when it comes to muscle building – that's the niche he owns.

But he diversifies by generating revenue with info products, a membership site, his original product "Muscle Gaining Secrets," running his Renegade Gym, and writing for Men's Fitness.

Brian Grasso is focused on the youth market, but generates revenue with writing, speaking, creating products, coaching programs, the IYCA, and our new franchise Athletic Revolution.

Lee Taft is the "speed guy" but not only does he have a facility, but he also has a bunch of products, has a certification with the IYCA, speaks, and has a membership program.

Dave Schmitz is the "band man" but generates revenue with his camps, working with athletes, offering information products educating on band training, speaking, and actually with his own line of bands and accessories.

Paul Reddick has baseball camps but also has a variety of products and continuity programs.

Holly has her main mom's fitness product – Fit Yummy Mummy – but also has a membership site, a DVD of the Month program, a DVD set, 2 other products, and also sells supplements to her FYMs.

So hopefully you see what I mean when I say focus and diversify.

Find your niche, and do your best to "own" it.

Then develop multiple revenue streams within that niche.

All I Got Was This Lousy T-Shirt?

I remember one day where we generated 48 new leads for our health club without any expensive newspaper or radio ads and without a member appreciation event or even a referral contest.

We got 48 new leads for around 8 T-Shirts. (It might have been 9... I'm not sure.) But let me back up a second.

I was talking with our Club Manager Lisa, and we were trying to decide the best approach to ask our current members for referrals.

We run a variety of referral systems, all with success, but the most effective is when we simply ask our new members to give us the names of friends and family members we can offer a free trial. So we decided to try to do the same with existing members, but we needed a "hook" to get them to give us the names.

Enter the T-Shirts.

Lisa and I decided that we would offer our members a T-Shirt in exchange for giving us names and contact information of people who they felt would benefit and appreciate a free trial to our club. So we ordered up some T-Shirts. When the T-shirts came in, we simply posted the offer on a dry erase board in the front of the club so that members would see it when they entered.

The result: 48 new leads on day one.

All for a few T-Shirts... that cost us about $5 each.

Maybe you ought to go order some T-Shirts.

The Easiest Profit Center to Add
On to Any Personal Training Business

Everyone wants multiple streams of income. The good news is that adding revenue streams to your business is easier than you think. If you have a handful of clients or a few people in your database, you can add another revenue stream to your business almost right away.

But instead of just telling you what that additional profit center is, I'm going to show you step-by-step how to implement it in your business.

The Weight Management Program – As a fitness professional you're well versed in the role nutrition plays in client success, so a weight management program is a natural fit. We began running weight management programs in our own business about 4 months after we opened, not fully knowing what to expect, and the results were incredible. The first month we sold over $5000 worth of weight management programs, not to mention the additional sales of meal replacement and other supplements that it led to – as well as more training sales.

For us, adding a weight management program easily increased our monthly revenue by 25%, and it can do the same for you – so here is your step by step plan:

Step 1: Decide Your Format – We started our program offering 1 on 1 sessions that were 30 minutes long where one of our coaches met with the client once a week for 10 weeks. Over time we tested 4, 8, 10, 12, and 16 week programs – both delivered 1 on 1 and in groups. We eventually found that for us, 12 week group programs or 4 week 1 on 1 programs were best.

The 12 week group format allowed us to break the program fee up into 3 monthly payments and let us better leverage our best weight management coach (Holly). The 4 week 1 on 1 program was an alternative we could sell at a higher per session price point to those people who couldn't make our group classes.

Step 2: Figure Out The Logistics – You need to decide where you will deliver the program, what you will include, and how much you will charge and when you will offer it.

If you have your own facility, the "where" is easy. If not, you may have to get creative. In most communities, you can get a small conference room inexpensively at a variety of places. Ask the local library, community center, and members of your personal network first.

The program could also be delivered using a service like Go To Webinar or Instant Teleseminar if you can't find a suitable space or simply choose not to.

As far as pricing goes – the easiest way to set the price is to match or slightly exceed what you'd charge for the same time commitment for group training or bootcamps (if you are delivering it in a group format). Or you can match your 1 on 1 training rates if you're delivering it individually.

So if you normally would charge someone $199 for 12 sessions of bootcamp, then at minimum, you should be charging that for your weight management program. However, because it's a one time program, you can charge more if you like. We typically charged $297 for our programs but we occasionally offered them for $199 as special offers to our clients.

What you will provide is relatively simple. We used a handbook that contained all 12 lessons plus weekly homework, a few one page handouts, and weekly emails to keep the students on track. You can find and dowload for free the exact resources we used at *nutritionmoneymachine.com*. It really is as easy and free as it sounds.

When you will offer the program depends on a few variables:

- Where will you be offering the classes?
- What else are you doing?
- What time of year is it?

My suggestion is to pick times that fall right after sessions or camps if you can. For us, some of the best time slots were:

➢ Monday – Thursday at 7 p.m.

➢ Any weekday at 10 a.m.

➢ Saturday morning at 10 a.m.

Remember, finding the perfect time isn't as important with this as it is with something like a bootcamp since it's only 1 day per week.

As far as what time of year – the season we found challenging was the time between Thanksgiving and Christmas. During the summer there was the occasional vacation, but a personal 15 minute call with the student to cover what they'd miss was more than enough to overcome that.

Step 3: Marketing The Program – The easiest people to market the program to are your current clients. Tell them that you're launching a new program, and you'll be limiting the first class to 12 people. Also tell them that you want to make it available first to your current clients before you open it to the public. Odds are, you'll fill up all 12 slots only presenting it to them.

If you don't fill up the program through **personal offers** to your current clients or if you choose to go beyond one class to start, individually contact former clients and unconverted leads.

Outside of those groups, you can market this program virtually the same way you'd market your training business. A couple of things to remember:

• Most/all of your students will be women so focus your marketing efforts there.

• This type of program will allow you to reach the Weight Watchers, Jenny Craig, NutriSystems and Curves audiences that may not necessarily be interested in your training offerings. This means that weight management programs can often be good front end programs to get people into your training programs.

Step 4: Delivering The Program – I won't spend too much time on this since you can get all the materials and the course outline free from the website I provided you with.

- Group sessions should last about an hour, while 1 on 1 will be less than 30 minutes.

- Begin each session with a recap of the previous session, go over the homework from the previous session, and address any questions the students may have over the material previously covered.

- Next, cover the lesson for the week. Deliver the content and answer questions the students have to provide clarity.

- Finish with a homework assignment related to the material covered.

Tips For Success – Here are a few tips to make the most of the program:

- Take before and after photos of all participants. This will be your most powerful marketing tool moving forward.

- Take the following measurements every 4 weeks: percent bodyfat, circumference, and weight. It is important to have accountability.

- Provide at least some sort of general exercise programming for the people who aren't currently training clients, and get them involved in a free trial of what you offer.

- In addition to the lesson related homework, have your students hold themselves accountable for a couple weekly goals like, "I will take my VGF consistently between now and next class," or, "I will drink 64 ounces of water daily between now and the next class." By saying this publicly in front of the group, they are more likely to follow through.

- Be a problem solver. If a student struggles with eating a supportive breakfast – provide a solution. If they eat out too often – provide a solution. If you give them simple solutions, you'll be amazed at the progress they can make in 12 weeks.

That's it – a simple program that you can use to add 10, 20, or even 30% to your monthly revenue. Plus, if you sell supplements, you'll see your sales go up significantly, as these people will become your best customers. And best of all, you'll find these clients have the highest lifetime value of anyone you work with because they get the best results, learn the most, and are the most connected to you.

Fool's Gold

The following is a story from Ryan Lee's Continuity Summit. This was a great event with a ton of information; however, while I was there, my biggest pet peeve reared its head too.

We went through a "speed networking" session that Ryan put together where you meet with a bunch of people in a hurry, and everyone shares their elevator pitches.

Well, about 5 out of the first 6 people who I met said stuff like, "I'm a list building expert, and I help people build huge lists."

So naturally I would respond with something like, "So how big is your list?"

"Well...ummmm...I'm just getting started."

Ugggghhhh.

I don't know about you, but I have a hard time swallowing the whole "expert" thing with people who don't actually practice what they preach.

You see it online a lot. People sell money making products and programs that supposedly teach you how to build a business online who have never built a business doing anything, yet they promise the get rich quick dream to naïve people.

But it's not exclusive to the money making market.

Have you seen all the people online who have a magic program promising to help everyone and anyone lose weight or build muscle – where the supposed "expert author" has never trained anyone except himself or his mom?

It's amazing.

I guess that in my "perfect world," if you tout yourself as an expert in anything, you should have some significant practical experience.

Trainers who don't take care of themselves probably shouldn't coach others. I'm not saying that they need to be cover model fit – but 75 pounds overweight is not acceptable.

List building "experts" should have built their own list.

Money making "experts" should be making money – not just selling money making info.

In fact, if the stuff they taught worked so well, why wouldn't they be practicing what they preach?

Nick and I still own a health club in large part to the fact that we buy in to that philosophy. Practice what you preach.

In fact, our entire business model for our Athletic Revolution franchise is based on only making money if our franchisees make money.

We're paid on a percentage.

If what we teach doesn't work – we're not profitable.

So do me a favor – before you package the world's best list building system – build your own list.

Before you become a business expert – run a successful business like the one you claim to be the "guru" for.

Before you launch the latest, greatest fat loss system – help hundreds or thousands of people lose fat in person.

I hate to rain on people's parades because I love catchy marketing as much as the next person, but the truth is – if it sounds too good to be true it is.

The 4 Hour Workweek is a lie – because NO ONE successful works four hours a week.

So commit to doing the work – but do it smart and efficiently so you reach your goals as quickly as possible – and do a great job.

Then market what you do.

Sell the sizzle, but actually deliver the steak.

Lessons I Learned From
Competitive Athletics

Where did you learn what it takes to be successful?

For me – outside of what my parents taught me – competitive sports had by far the biggest impact.

It's funny, thinking back to the things I learned in high school, as an undergrad, and in graduate school – not a lot of it has a daily impact on what I do.

But the lessons I learned in sports – they matter every day.

Here are a few of the things being an athlete or coaching athletes taught me:

- **The Ability To Handle Adversity** – You can't go very far as an athlete without having to overcome adversity, and the most successful athletes are usually the ones who deal with adversity the most effectively.

- **Work Ethic** – I remember my freshman year of high school going to baseball practice at 3:15 after school and being done at 8. It was kind of a rude awakening for a 14 year old, but I quickly learned that to be successful you couldn't do just enough to get by. I don't know anyone who has ever become a real success just punching the clock and working 9-5.

- **The Intangibles Matter As Much As The Tangibles** – Many of the most talented athletes I've ever played with or coached were huge underachievers when it came to performance. They didn't have the passion, drive, or willingness to work hard. They couldn't handle adversity. To this day – I'll hire intangibles 10 times out of 10 over a great resume.

- **To Keep Score** – The beauty of sports is that you keep score. There is a tangible way to measure performance. I tracked everything as a coach because I was looking for an edge. We track our numbers for the same reasons now; if you don't keep score, you cannot measure how you're performing and know where to focus your efforts on improvement.

- **Sacrifice & A Team Attitude** – If you compete in a team sport and want to succeed at a high level, you quickly learn to work within the framework of a group, sacrifice some of your individual goals for the good of the team, and understand that if you want to be a champion you need to get past selfishness and shortsightedness.

- **You Can't Hide** – In baseball, when you step in the batter's box it's a moment of truth. You either put in the hours or you didn't. As a coach, when your team takes the field, you either recruited and did the job preparing your team, or you didn't. Too many people make excuses. Sports teach you that excuses don't get you very far.

- **Hustle Can Make Up For A Lot** – As a player I got to play at a higher level than my talent probably would have taken me because I worked hard. As a coach we developed a nationally ranked program with some of the worst resources in the country. If you're willing to outwork the competition, you will be able to overcome a lot of shortcomings – whether it is talent, resources, or anything else.

That's just a sample of the things being involved in competitive athletics taught me. If you were involved in sports – what did they teach you?

5 Rules To Live By In Business

Coaches love quotes and clichés.

It's almost impossible to find a coach that doesn't have quotes or clichés all over his office or locker room.

I was no exception.

I love distilling things down – a checklist to teach a system or a sentence that conveys a bigger message.

So here are 5 of my favorite rules for business and a sentence or two about what they mean:

1. **You get paid for done.** You don't get anything for having a great idea, getting started, or developing a plan. The finish is what matters. You only reap rewards when you get done.

2. **Be remarkable.** No one raves about ordinary. Deliver an extraordinary experience and a caliber of service that people can't help but talk about, and everything else about business becomes much, much easier.

3. **Never stop learning.** At every seminar I've ever been to, the most successful people always

seemed to be asking questions and taking notes. This is not an accident.

4. **One is the loneliest number.** Only one revenue stream and you're only a couple of steps away from disaster. Only one team member means no time off and a lot of time working on things you don't enjoy working on.

5. **Treat everyone like a prospect. Treat every prospect like a client. Treat every client like they're family. Treat your family (and business family) like gold.** As far as I'm concerned, relationships are everything. Grow your relationships, and you'll also be growing your business.

There are 5 of my favorite business lessons – all worthy of their own posters.

Fitness Industry Problems:
An Opportunity For You

No matter what industry you're in, problems create opportunities.

Walt Disney developed Disneyland in response to the fact that amusement parks left a lot to be desired.

Wal-Mart grew like crazy because retailers ignored markets outside the big cities.

If most of the fitness industry is going to ignore the problems at hand, then that equates to opportunities for you. Here are the most obvious opportunities as I see them:

Become "The Solution" For a Targeted Group of People In Your Area – In Boston, baseball players seek out Eric Cressey's gym. In Edison, NJ, wrestlers flock to Zach Even-Esh's Underground Gym. If you're in Santa Clarita and want to lose fat, you go to the Cosgrove's gym. If you want sports performance training in Watchung, NJ, Jason Ferruggia's Renegade Gym is the go to solution. In Pembroke, MA, young athletes seek out Dave & Andrea Gleason's Athletic Revolution.

Determine who you want to serve and become the "go to solution" for that group. I know these people all built businesses by becoming passionate about helping a certain group and putting in the time to become the best solution for that audience.

If you take this approach as a businessperson, everything becomes easier. You know what you have to focus on, what to study, who to market to, and what your identity is.

I really think that the fitness industry is poised to move this way – targeted solutions for specific audiences. It's up to you whether you'll be one of the leaders.

Build a Community – All the gyms I just mentioned have their own community. Starbucks coined the idea of becoming their customers' 3rd place – that place people wanted to be outside of home and work.

Great fitness businesses become that 3rd place for their clients.

I mentioned it before. I don't care if you love or hate CrossFit, but they've built a community. Their members are posting pics and videos all over their Facebook pages, communicating with other "CrossFitters" outside the gym and making their experience viral. Think that stuff happens at Bally's?

Find ways to connect your clients with one another. Encourage them to support each other. Instead of each client only being "your client" – they also become part of "your team" or "your family."

Do that and you'll be amazed at the impact on your business, and you'll separate yourself from all the other trainers and gyms in your area.

Be The Anti-Health Club – Even if you are a health club. Make everything personal. Know your clients... not just their names. Know about their work, their families, and their hobbies. Even if you run group classes or bootcamps, at least spend some one-on-one time with clients in the beginning to build relationships and learn about them. Then make it a priority to have periodic one-on-one contact with them regularly.

If other clubs want to try to be Wal Mart, then you can be the boutique location that everyone raves about.

Deliver Results or Find a Different Career – If you aren't focused on making the people you work with better, move on. You aren't doing yourself or anybody else any favors if you don't deliver results.

I've spent a LOT of time in health club settings, and most trainers there don't work to improve at their craft, don't do assessments, don't design programs, and don't really care about their clients.

They just sell training and give workouts.

Take the complete opposite approach.

Study like crazy. Become a great trainer or coach, and accept that it will require a BIG investment (time and money) on your part to get there.

Do assessments, design programs, and care about your clients' success. Focus on delivering results.

If you happen to work in a big gym, then do this, and you'll quickly set yourself apart from 99% of the other trainers there.

Run A Business That's Tough To Beat – If you're going to be part of the solution in the fitness industry as an entrepreneur, that means you are going to have to run a sound business that's poised to compete successfully with the big box health clubs. Here are the components I think give you the best chance for success:

- A facility with a low overhead, having primarily an open floor plan without expensive cardio machines or selectorized equipment.

- A model primarily based around group training.

- A specific target market (or two) that you're trying to serve.

- The utilization of EFT billing.

- A dedication to having a community atmosphere.

- A focus on client results instead of client volume.

- Several different revenue streams.

All the businesses that I mentioned previously utilize most, if not all, of these components. Our new youth fitness and athletic performance franchise, Athletic Revolution, incorporates all of these components.

They give you the best chance for success.

So where do bootcamps fall into this plan? Other than the facility, they fit the bill to a "T". It's beyond the scope of this post to compare bootcamps where the owners have their own space versus ones where the owner uses someone else's space, but I will say that controlling your own space certainly has advantages over being at someone else's mercy.

So there you have it – my formula for taking advantage of the problems the fitness industry currently faces. What do you think? Are you one of the leaders ready to step up and take advantage of the opportunities I've mentioned?

Do You Have At Least 5 Of These?

If you want to build a business that is resistant to struggle, then I think you should have at least 5 different revenue streams. How many do you have?

Here are 21 that you can choose from "a la carte" style:

- One-on-One Training
- Semi-Private Training or Small Group Training (2-4 Clients)
- Large Group Training (5-10 Clients)
- Bootcamps
- Youth Fitness Programs
- Sports Performance Programs
- Nutrition or Weight Management Programs
- Fitness Coaching Programs
- Corporate Fitness Programs or Bootcamps
- Supplements
- Sports Performance Clinics and Camps

- Short Term Programs – like our 21 Day Drop a Dress Size Program
- DVDs that you produce
- Books or E-Books that you write
- Transformation or other Contests
- "Tools" – Guys like Dave Schmitz at *Resistance Band Training* have great affiliate programs you can sell
- Paid Seminars and Workshops
- "Off Day Programs" – either live or by selling clients **Workout Muse Interval Tracks**
- Certification Workshops or other paid events
- Affiliate products and programs you believe in that you can promote in your newsletter
- Niche Specific Programs – Moms, Brides, Diabetics, Baby Boomers, Seasonal, Short Term, etc.

That's a pretty long list, but it's just scratching the surface.

Epilogue

What's Next?

I've covered a lot of territory in this book, and you probably have a lot of ideas to get started. But you may also have a pretty long list of question marks like, "How do I do that?"

When Nick and I first started out, we asked that same question many times. Over the years, we have built a huge arsenal of tools, resources, experts, and vendors. All of these make it much, much easier to do what you do.

As a reader, you can see all of these at our "hub" site, Fit Business Insider. Just visit

www.FitBusinessInsider.com

to find a knowledge base of everything you need to take your business to the next level.

The Most Incredible

FREE Gift Ever

Over $500 Worth Of Fitness Business Building Information

Pat Rigsby & Nick Berry are offering an incredible opportunity for you to see why Fit Business Insider is THE Place where entrepreneurial fitness professionals go for Fast & Dramatic Business Growth and Financial & Personal Independence. Pat & Nick want to give you over $500 worth of Fitness Business Building Information including a FREE Month as a Gold Member of the Fit Business Inner Circle.

Your Gift Includes:

The Six Figure Code (Valued at $97) – The simple Six Step System for propelling your business to $100,000 a year and beyond.

The Referral Manual (Valued at $27)– This e-book is the definitive guide on generating referrals for personal trainers and bootcamp owners.

Building a $25,000 a Month Personal Training Business On A Shoestring Budget (Valued at $397)– This collection of audios and transcripts reveal how Pat

& Nick built a $25,000 a month training business in less than 12 months starting with less than $2000.

Low Cost Fitness Marketing (Valued at $47)– This Video Training reveals the key low cost marketing strategies fitness professionals can use to explode their businesses.

Tapping Into Your Fitness Gold Mine (Valued at $47)– This Video Training will teach you over a dozen different strategies you can use to tap into profit centers that you've missed before but are right there for the taking.

Gold Level Fit Business Inner Circle Membership (One Month Value - $47)– This Online Membership will teach you What's Working Now in the industry. Marketing, Sales, Infoproduct Creation, Trends and More.

To Activate Your MOST INCREDIBLE FREE GIFT EVER, you just need to go to:

www.FitBusinessInsider.com/book

There you will create your Username and Password to gain access to over $500 worth of Business Building and Profit Producing Information.

Will You Do Me A Favor?

So you've read the book, and now I'm wondering if you would take a few minutes to post a comment on the blog at www.FitBusinessInsider.com where you can share your thoughts about what you learned and how it can or has impacted you and your business.

We and other fitness entrepreneurs want to know what you think about it! All you need to do is go to www.FitBusinessInsider.com and leave a comment on any blog post. And if you leave your email address I'll send you a bonus gift to show my appreciation.

I really appreciate your help, and we look forward to personally seeing your feedback.

Dedicated To Your Success,

Pat

About The Author

Pat Rigsby is an author, consultant, and fitness entrepreneur and is the co-owner of over a dozen businesses within the fitness industry. He, along with Nick Berry, has positioned Fitness Consulting Group as the leading business development organization in the fitness industry. FCG provides resources, coaching programs, and consulting to give you everything you need to start or grow your personal training or fitness related business.

In addition to his business coaching and consulting work, Pat is also the co-owner of two of the leading fitness franchises in the world, Athletic Revolution and Fitness Revolution.

Athletic Revolution, the fastest growing youth fitness and sports performance franchise in the world, was founded in order to provide passionate youth fitness professionals with a system for developing a successful business that could provide them with a fulfilling career and a chance to have a profound impact in their communities serving the youth market. You can learn more about the Athletic Revolution opportunity by visiting:

www.MyAthleticRevolution.com

Fitness Revolution, launched in January, 2011, is already the fastest growing personal training franchise in the world. It was developed to allow the fitness industry's best trainers and coaches to have access to the systems, tools, and support necessary to reach their professional potential. You can learn more about the Fitness Revolution opportunity by going to:

www.FitnessRevolutionFranchise.com.

Pat also hosts a number of conferences and webinars and writes a blog and newsletter that reach over 65,000 fitness professionals on the topics of fitness business development, fitness marketing, and other business topics. He has been seen on NBC, ABC, CBS, and in industry publications like Personal Fitness Professional, Club Industry and Club Business International. You can learn more about Pat's coaching programs and products or download his collection of free business building gifts by going to www.FitBusinessInsider.com.

Made in the USA
Middletown, DE
16 June 2016